# Infant
# Development

**MARGARET B. PUCKETT**
*Texas Wesleyan University*

**JANET K. BLACK**
*Texas A&M University*

These chapters are
reprinted from
# The Young Child:
## Development from Prebirth Through Age Eight,

Third Edition, by Margaret B. Puckett
and Janet K. Black,
©2001 by Prentice-Hall, Inc.

Merrill
Prentice Hall

Upper Saddle River, New Jersey
Columbus, Ohio

**Vice President and Publisher:** Jeffery W. Johnston
**Executive Editor:** Kevin M. Davis
**Associate Editor:** Christina Tawney
**Development Editor:** Julie Peters
**Editorial Assistant:** Autumn Crisp
**Production Editor:** Mary Harlan
**Design Coordinator:** Diane C. Lorenzo
**Photo Coordinator:** Nancy Ritz/Carol Sykes
**Production Manager:** Laura Messerly
**Director of Marketing:** Ann Castel Davis
**Marketing Manager:** Amy June
**Marketing Coordinator:** Tyra Cooper

**Photo Credits:** Nancy P. Alexander: pp. 25, 29, 36, 45, 49, 58, 67, 87; Michael Newman/Photo Edit: p. 77; Margaret B. Puckett: pp. 15, 20, 81, 94.

Merrill
Prentice Hall

10 9 8 7 6 5 4 3 2 1
ISBN: 0-13-098643-7

# Infant Development

# CHAPTER FIVE

# Physical and Motor Development of the Infant

*Infancy conforms to nobody—all conform to it.*

RALPH WALDO EMERSON

---

*After studying this chapter, you will demonstrate comprehension by:*

▶ Describing sociocultural influences on prenatal and infant growth and development.

▶ Outlining principles of development related to the physical and motor development of infants from birth to the end of the first year.

▶ Describing earliest brain growth and neurological development.

▶ Describing major physiological competencies of the infant.

▶ Explaining expected patterns of physical and motor development during the first year.

▶ Identifying major factors influencing physical and motor development.

▶ Suggesting strategies for promoting and enhancing physical and motor development during the first year.

▶ Discussing contemporary infant health and well-being issues.

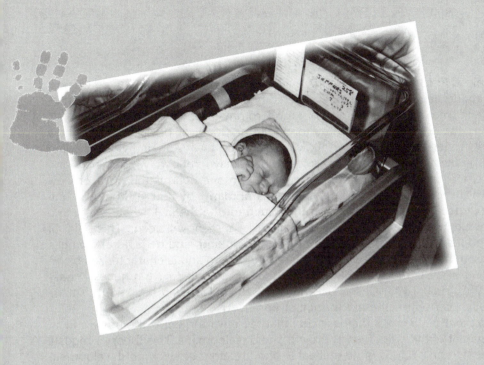

*To make room* for incoming expectant mothers in the prenatal care unit, Cheryl has been moved to a semiprivate room down the hall. Between school and work schedules, James has tried to be with Cheryl as much as possible. Today, members of her large extended family and one or two of her close friends have gather eagerly around Cheryl in the hospital room to share in the joy of Angela's birth. Since Angela is receiving special attention in the neonatal intensive care unit, they are also concerned for her well-being. Family and friends stroll quietly into and out of Cheryl's room, returning from viewing the newborn through a window to the neonatal intensive care unit. They share their observations and excitement: "She's so beautiful, so tiny." "She was awake and squirming. I believe she has James's eyes; I always thought James and his brother had those same beautiful eyes." "She seems a little upset with all those nurses fussing over her." "Cheryl was a calm and easy baby" muses her mother. "I remember Cheryl being a crybaby when she was little," chirps one of her siblings. "No, you were the crybaby, not me," quips Cheryl in characteristic sibling retort. Happy banter continues among Cheryl and her friends and family: "Will Angela have musical ability and like to sing like Cheryl always did?" "Cheryl, are you going to sing to your baby?" "Will she have James's personality and charm, his energy, or his ability in games and sports?" "She is so tiny, will she be normal and healthy?"

## PRINCIPLES OF GROWTH, DEVELOPMENT, AND BEHAVIOR

These observations and conversations about a newborn child are typical and suggest curiosity about what gives each child his or her unique characteristics and traits. They illustrate an old debate over the relative importance of heredity and environment in a child's uniqueness. For instance, we can all agree that eye color is genetically determined and is not altered by environmental influences. But can we all agree that an infant's motor skills are genetically

3

determined and unalterable through environmental influences? What do we now know about the relative influence of heredity and environment (nature and nurture), and what are we learning from modern day science?

Over the years, theorists have provided a variety of perspectives on how growth proceeds and why it follows certain pathways in individuals, what causes individuals to behave in unique and idiosyncratic ways, and how and why certain capabilities and talents emerge. On one hand is the point of view that growth and development are controlled primarily by nature (heredity) and are governed by an inborn, unalterable blueprint that defines what, when, and to what extent each aspect of growth and development will occur. This point of view proposes that all growth, development, thinking, and behavioral changes result from maturation occurring within the organism and is characterized by an unfolding of traits along predictable time lines controlled by the genes (Anastasi, 1958; Hall, 1893; Gesell & Amatruda, 1941; Gesell & Ilg, 1949). This is generally referred to as a **maturationist perspective.**

On the other hand is the assertion that the environment is the more critical determinant of the outcomes of growth and development. This theory suggests that the human being is quite malleable and therefore growth and development are facilitated or impeded by influences in the individual's environment (Bandura, 1977, 1986; Bijou & Baer, 1961; Skinner, 1974; J. B. Watson, 1924). This **behaviorist perspective** asserts that the environment shapes developmental outcomes regardless of genetic makeup. Consequently, where the environment provides appropriate experiences (i.e., instruction, educational opportunities, praise, punishment, reinforcement, support, neglect), the outcomes for the individual can be externally influenced.

Piaget's (1952) **developmental interactionist perspective** on cognitive development challenged the notions that growth and development are at the mercy of the individual's genes and that growth, development and learning are acquired primarily through experience and reinforcement techniques. Rather, he hypothesized that children are born with certain abilities that can flourish when supported by a rich and engaging environment. The individual is thought to construct knowledge within his or her own mind as a consequence of physical and mental interactions with objects, situations, and people. His theory suggests that environments that provide limited stimulation and mental engagement actually impede optimal growth and learning.

Still others proposes a **transactional perspective** in which one's inherited attributes and environmental experiences influence one another through an ongoing interplay between heredity and environment (Sameroff, 1983; Sameroff & Chandler, 1975). The transactional perspective says that inherited characteristics are shaped by experience and that experience is shaped by inherited traits. The interplay and interdependence between nature and nurture proceed in a mutual give-and-take manner throughout the life span of the individual. This perspective has made a major contribution to the study of human growth and development, for it suggests that as development proceeds, new characteristics or traits that are not present in the original fertilized egg may well emerge as a result of transactions between heredity and environment. For example, a child who is, by nature, slow to warm up to others may encounter an environment in which caregivers are sensitive and supportive increasing the child's ability to trust and relate more readily to others. Slowly, over time, this inherent trait, while still present, may be mediated by relationships that facilitate interactions with others.

**maturationist perspective:** the point of view that growth and development are primarily governed by an individual's genetic makeup.

**behaviorist perspective:** the point of view that growth and development are primarily governed by external influences in the individual's environment.

**developmental interactionist perspective:** the point of view that growth and development result from an individual's actions within and upon the environment.

**transactional perspective:** the point of view that growth and development are an outgrowth of the interplay between an individual's heredity and environment

**Bidirectional Influences**

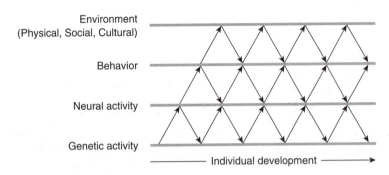

**FIGURE 5.1**
Depiction of the completely bidirectional nature of genetic, neural, behavioral, and environmental influences over the course of individual development.

*Source:* Individual Development and Evolution: The Genesis of Novel Behavior *by Gilbert Gottlieb, Copyright © 1991 by Oxford University Press, Inc. Used by permission of Oxford University Press, Inc.)*

An elaboration of this transactional model is proposed by Gottlieb, (1995, 1992), in which he describes a multilevel system that incorporates the interplay of "culture, society, immediate social and physical environments, anatomy, physiology, hormones, cytoplasm, and genes" (1995, p. 137). The interactions among these influences are bidirectional, and genes are considered not directors outside the system, dictating the course of development, but active players in a complex system of give and take. Gottlieb's theory joins a contemporary genre referred to as a **systems approach** to understanding growth, development, and learning. Figure 5.1 illustrates Gottlieb's bidirectional model.

Perhaps the best-known systems approach to understanding child growth, development, and learning is the theory set forth by Urie Bronfenbrenner (1979, 1986). Recall from Chapter 1 that Bronfenbrenner proposed an ecological systems theory that describes various spheres of influence in a number of systems or contexts interacting on one another and with the child (see Figure 1.3). A systems approach to the study of child growth, development, and learning allows for consideration of influences associated with race and ethnicity, cultural and faith-related values, traditions, belief systems, socioeconomic circumstances, gender influences, and numerous networks of relationships heretofore unsatisfactorily addressed by other theories.

For example, family and culture groups hold varying assumptions about when independent mobility (crawling, walking) should begin and how it can be encouraged. Some cultural groups encourage early walking by providing infants with greater or lesser freedom of movement. Some cultures keep infants tightly swaddled, perhaps carried about on their mothers' sides or backs during most of the early months. Still others restrict infants' explorations to designated spaces, such as a playpen, a gated child's room, or another specified play area. Still others provide free-range use of the environment for exploration through rolling over, crawling, pulling up, and walking and the use of special toys and equipment to encourage motor development. This is common in Western cultures, in which all sorts of commercial products such as floor mats, baby swings, pull and push toys, climbing toys, and other devices are popular among parents and caregivers. These simple differences in early child rearing result in slightly different timetables for the onset of walking and other motor abilities, though humans are genetically programmed for coordination, movement, and mobility. Differences in emergence of particular skills are viewed as simply that—different, neither superior nor inferior, normal nor abnormal. This

**systems approach:** an ecological perspective on growth and development that considers the many layers of influence between and among different contexts in which the individual exists.

perspective allows us to look at individual children in holistic ways that appreciate uniqueness and individuality.

## FORMULATING A FRAMEWORK FOR UNDERSTANDING CHILD GROWTH, DEVELOPMENT, AND LEARNING

In the process of formulating a framework for understanding child growth and development, early childhood professionals draw prominent concepts from all of the theories. It is probably fair to say, that in practice (parenting, child care, teaching, and policy development), elements of all of the theories come into play. Hence, we are guided by a number of basic principles of growth, development, and learning that are drawn from a variety of theoretic perspectives (maturationists, behaviorists, interactionists, transactionist, and contextualistic). The following principles are thought to be generally true for all growth and development and to transcend, for the most part, race and geography.

1. *Growth and development depend on an intricate interplay among and between heredity and environmental influences.* Individual differences among children are attributed to an array of influences related to biology and the physiological integrity of the human organism itself and the contexts and types of experiences to which an individual is exposed.

2. *Physical growth and development generally follow a* **cephalocaudal** *and* **proximodistal** *direction.* That is, growth and development proceed from the head downward and from the central axis of the body outward. Dramatic neurological development and brain growth take place during prenatal development and the first three years of life. This is evident in the bodily proportions of the newborn. The newborn is quite top-heavy, the head accounting for one-quarter of the total body length. These proportions are illustrated in Figure 5.2.

   This law of developmental direction applies not only to body proportions but also to other forms of development. It is most obvious in the development and coordination of large and small muscles. Coordination of the large muscles of the upper body, including the neck, shoulders, upper trunk, and upper arms, generally precedes coordination of the smaller muscles in those body regions. Also, throughout infancy and early childhood, the muscles of the upper body become more mature and coordinated than those of the lower regions of the body, with the large muscles of the hips and upper legs developing before the smaller muscles of the lower legs, ankles, and feet.

3. *Most children follow similar developmental patterns.* As a rule, one stage of the pattern paves the way for the next. In motor development, for instance, a predictable sequence of development precedes walking. Infants lift and turn their heads before they turn over and are able to move their arms and legs before grasping an object.

4. *There are critical periods during growth and development in which the child is physically and psychologically more sensitive and vulnerable to environmental influences and social/emotional interactions.* During these periods, the child is susceptible to both positive and negative experiences that

**cephalocaudal:** refers to the long axis of the body from the head downward

**proximodistal:** refers to the direction from the body's center outward to the extremities

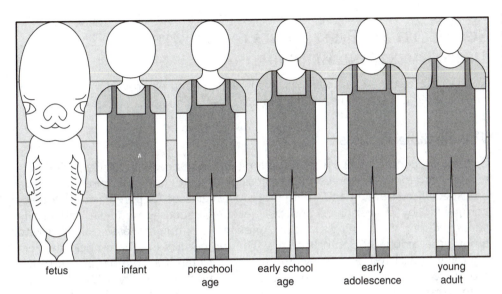

**FIGURE 5.2**
Cephalocaudal Direction of Growth and Development

At birth, the newborn's head is 70 percent of its eventual adult size.

| fetus | infant | preschool age | early school age | early adolescence | young adult |

can either enhance or impede the growth process. Indeed, contemporary studies of neurological development and brain growth emphasize the fact that there are prime times for optimal development.

5. *There are individual rates of growth and development.* While the patterns or sequences for growth and development are similar among children, the rates at which individual children reach specific developmental milestones vary. For example, one child may begin walking unassisted at 9 months; another may begin at 15 months. Also, for most children, physiological growth occurs in spurts, but for some, growth appears to occur in steady increments. A significant example of variance in individual rates of growth is in the manner in which children become literate. Contrary to prevalent assumptions that literacy must be taught at a certain age and through certain methodologies, literacy development has its origins in infancy and emerges through varied processes and at different rates among children of the same chronological age.

6. *Rates of development are not uniform among developmental domains in individual children.* For instance, a child's intellectual development may outpace his or her emotional or social development. Another child may show precocious motor skills but less sophisticated skill in the use of language.

7. *Throughout the life span, an individual's growth, development, learning, and behaviors are influenced by cultural and societal contexts.* The cultural and societal contexts in which individuals grow and develop encompass numerous elements that influence and determine unique developmental pathways and outcomes: availability of nutritious foods and family food preferences and meal patterns; health care practices; faith-based activities and belief systems; family composition, goals, values, and priorities; daily routines and responsibilities; family and community economic resources; access to educational opportunities; education level of family members; community characteristics which include adequate and comfortable housing, recreational facilities, employment, and family enrichment opportunities; and the prevailing political climate of the community and nation.

# SOCIOCULTURAL PERSPECTIVES ON GROWTH, DEVELOPMENT, AND BEHAVIOR

Following are some examples of ways in which cultures around the world vary in their child development beliefs and practices.

## The Birthing Process

Birthing procedures range from no or limited assistance from family and friends to high-technology hospitals with professional health care personnel who have had specialized training and where preparation classes for parents-to-be are accompanied by philosophies and policies that encourage spouse and family support during the birthing process. An example of minimal assistance is found among the Siriono of South America. The mother lies in a hammock, delivers the baby unassisted, and allows the newborn to fall from the hammock to the ground, a procedure that is thought to stimulate the birth cry. Although many of the women in the community gather around to keep the birth mother company, they make no attempt to assist her. This practice differs appreciably from hospital or at-home deliveries assisted by a certified nurse-midwife or possibly a nonprofessional midwife and other family members. Home deliveries are popular in a number of countries, such as England, the Netherlands, and Sweden.

## Carrying, Cuddling, and Transporting the Infant

In the cultures of Africa, Asia, South America, and some other places, infants are carried about all day on their mothers' backs or in a sling or pouch at their mothers' sides while the mothers go about their daily chores. Infant and mother are virtually inseparable, and the infant is breast-fed on demand throughout the day. Some babies are carried this way until the age of two, three, or four; the arrival of a sibling usually necessitates the separation (Weisner, 1982).

In contrast, in Western cultures, babies are carried upright, peering over the shoulders of their parents or caregivers, and are often transported in a variety of devices such as strollers, baby carriages, and carrying seats of various types, such as pouches strapped across the shoulders and around the waist of the adult.

## Infant Crying

In some cultures, infants' cries are perceived as distress signals and are responded to readily with food, a pacifier, patting, or holding. In others, such as the United States, adults often take a wait- and see approach to determine the extent of the infant's distress and whether the baby is able to comfort itself and return to sleep. Japanese mothers often let their babies nestle in bed with them and cuddle and hold them until they fall back to sleep.

## Nonmaternal Child Care

North Americans and Europeans in the mid-twentieth century believed that mothers should not work but devote their time and energies to child rearing. Yet for many cultures today, particularly in industrialized and technological countries, nonmaternal child care and employed mothers are the norm. Nonmaternal child care is provided by the grandmother or another older female in the extended family for Chinese infants whose mothers return to work soon after the first month. Home care is preferred during the first year (Chance, 1984).

In some Native American tribes, all members of the family are expected to contribute to the maintenance and well-being of the family or group, regardless of the absence or presence of the mother. Grandmothers, aunts, male relatives, and other children may share responsibility for infants. Sometimes very young children (four and five years old) are expected to care for babies and toddlers (Locust, 1988). In the United States, Latino families are less likely to place their children in preschools, relying more frequently on family and friends when child care is needed (Fuller, Eggers-Pierola, Holloway, Liang, & Rambaud, 1995).

With these caveats about the wide ranges of experience and philosophy regarding child bearing and infancy, let us explore what contemporary scholars are learning about infant growth and development.

# BEGINNINGS: PHYSICAL AND MOTOR COMPETENCE OF THE NEWBORN

The newborn enters the world with impressive abilities. From intrauterine to extrauterine life, the newborn must make a number of physiological adjustments, including breathing, taking in nourishment, and eliminating body wastes. The newborn makes adjustments from being surrounded by the warm amniotic fluid of the uterine environment to being surrounded by air, which is dry and cool and fluctuates in temperature. The newborn also adjusts from an environment of limited sensory stimulation to an environment of many complex and varied stimuli that quicken all of the sensory mechanisms of sight, sound, smell, touch, taste, and **kinesthesis.** Despite seemingly overwhelming demands on the heretofore profoundly dependent organism, the infant emerges as a remarkably competent individual. Let's begin our discussion of the infant's competencies and potential with a description of early brain growth and neurological development.

**kinesthesis:**
the perception of movement

## Earliest Brain Growth and Neurological Development

During the first weeks of prenatal development, the **neural tube** (which will develop into the spinal column and brain) emerges out of the **embryonic cell mass.** Specific cells along the length of the tube develop into specific types of **neurons,** or nerve cells. During prenatal development, neurons are forming at a startling rate of 250,000 a minute. Neurons are tiny; it is estimated that 30,000 of them can fit into a space the size of a pinhead (Sylwester, 1995). The spinal column, brain, and a spectacular network of nerve cells make up the nervous system. The nervous system has three interrelated functions: "to receive and interpret information about the internal and external environment of the body, to make decisions about this information, and to organize and carry out action" based on this information (Delcomyn, 1998, p. 7).

The human organism has sophisticated capabilities for receiving and interpreting information about its internal and external environments through the

**neural tube:**
the rudimentary beginning of the brain and spinal cord

**embryonic cell mass:**
the developing fertilized ovum during the first three months of pregnancy when cells are dividing rapidly to form the fetus

**neuron:**
a type of cell that conveys information; a nerve cell

*sensory system,* which includes all of the sense organs of the body and sensory neurons that transport information from the sense organs to other parts of the nervous system. The *motor system,* includes the muscles, certain glands of the body, and the motor neurons that are needed to activate the muscles and glands. There is a third system in our sophisticated neurological makeup in which the complex task of taking information from the sensory system, accessing memory of previous experiences, and then making decisions about prior information stored in memory and the new information takes place. This system is referred to as the *integrating system* because it must coordinate and integrate many sources of information and many different parts of the nervous system. This activity is carried out by nerve cells called interneurons (Delcomyn, 1998).

Recent advances in technology, neuroscience, and medicine have made it possible to study with amazing precision the neurological system and the brain. Imaging technology such as *high-resolution ultrasound recordings,* a noninvasive technique that creates a sonogram picture of the fetus using sound waves, are used quite frequently now. *Computed axial tomography* (CT or CAT scan) is a noninvasive procedure that uses computers to provide multiple-angle pictures of the brain giving information about its structure. *Magnetic resonance imaging* (MRI), also a noninvasive technique, employs magnetic fields, radio frequencies, and computer technology to produce high-contrast images that allow scientists to examine various anatomical features of the brain. The *functional MRI* (fMRI) combines imaging of activity in the brain with MRI images of the brain's structure. The *positron emission tomography* (PET scan) uses radioactive dye, either injected or ingested, to view not only the structures of the brain, as with the CAT scan, but also complex neurological activity as it takes place in various parts of the brain. *Video-enhanced microscopy* combines microscopic images with video technology to examine the characteristics and activity of minute particles in living tissue. In addition to these remarkable imaging techniques, scientists now have methods to analyze the electrical and chemical activity in the brain and neurological system. For example, by analyzing levels of the hormone cortisol in saliva, the impact of adverse and stressful experiences on the brain can be estimated. Cortisol levels rise when stress increases, and we now know that persistent high levels of cortisol can be damaging to brain cells and have been associated with some developmental delays and neurological impairments (Gazzaniga, 1988, Vincent, 1990). Specialized studies such as these are yielding important information for the study of child development.

During the embryonic period, neural cells that will form the parts of the nervous system grow from germ cells, which divide repeatedly, generating new cells. This process of generating new cells ceases before an infant's birth. Hence, infants are born with a lifetime supply of nerve cells, or neurons—more than 100 billion, which have already formed more than 50 trillion connections. No new cells will ever develop, but these cell bodies will continue to grow **axons** (usually a single long fiber) that convey information *away* from the cell body) and **dendrites** (branches that convey information *toward* the cell body) that will travel in designated pathways to connect through a process called **synapse** to form a very dense and complex system of connections. Neurons communicate through this synapse either through certain chemicals known as **neurotransmitters** or by the transmission of electrical currents from one neuron

**axon:**
a branchlike projection from the neuron that carries information away from the cell body

**dendrites:**
branches from the neuron that carry information toward the cell body. A neuron can have several dendrites.

**synapse:**
the point at which adjacent nerve cells (neurons) transmit information

**neurotransmitter:**
a chemical response that facilitates the transmission of information through the synapse

to another. During infancy and the first year of development, these connections are bursting forth at an astounding rate. By the end of the infant's first year, the brain is two-thirds its adult size, and by the end of the second year, it will be about four-fifths of its adult size. Environmental sensory stimuli cause the brain to develop its own unique circuitry and determine which connections will last (or become "hard wired") and which connections will be so weak that they **atrophy** and die. Connections that are not used frequently enough are pruned away or sometimes rerouted to another compensating or perhaps less appropriate or debilitating connection. Studies of infants and young children who have not received healthy, consistent, predictable, repetitive sensory experiences during this critical period of growth and development have shown that they have significantly smaller brain sizes and abnormal brain development (Perry, 1998).

During the early growth of nerve cells, **myelin,** which is a fatty tissue made up of **glial** membrane, begins to wrap around the axon and dendrites. Myelin promotes the efficient transmission of messages along the neurons and strengthens synapses (see Figure 5.3). Its growth coincides with the development of vision and hearing systems, motor development, language, certain cognitive processes, and the expression and control of feelings and emotions. All experiences (or sensory input that the child receives) affects neurological development by strengthening the synapses. Over the life span of an individual, many nerve cells die as a consequence of the prenatal production of more cells than are actually needed or than can survive to adulthood and through lack of use. Consequently, reduction of number of neurons present at birth occurs throughout development, resulting at adulthood in half the original number of cells.

Of special interest to child developmentalists is the concept of windows of opportunity, which are identified periods during growth and development when certain synaptic activity can be strengthened if infants and young children are provided appropriate experiences. From recent studies of prenatal and infant neurological development and brain growth, it is now evident that the first three years are critical, particularly for the neurological development that is associated with attachment, control of emotions, and ability to cope with stress, vision, and motor development. Table 5.1 illustrates these windows of opportunity. With this brief synopsis of early neurological development and brain

**atrophy:**
wasting away, diminishing in size and function

**myelin:**
a fatty substance surrounding the axons and dendrites of some neurons that speeds the conduction of nerve impulses

**glial cells:**
supporting cells that serve to protect and insulate (as in myelin) cells in the nervous system

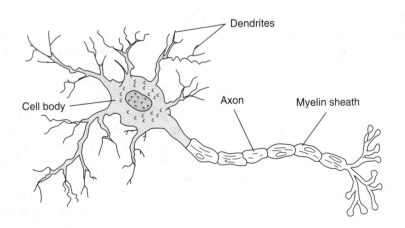

Cell body · Dendrites · Axon · Myelin sheath

**FIGURE 5.3**
Myelination of Nerve Cells

The growth of myelin, or fatty tissue, around the nerve cells of the brain coincides with development of the auditory system, rapid language development, and increased processing of visual, spatial, and temporal information.

| TABLE 5.1 | Windows of Opportunity in Early Brain Growth and Neurological Development |
|-----------|-----------------------------------------------------------------|

| Age | Developmental Domain |
|-----|---------------------|
| Birth to 2 years | Social attachment, ability to cope with stress |
| Birth to 3 years | Regulation of emotions |
| Birth to 2 years | Visual and auditory acuity |
| Birth to 3 years | Vocabulary |
| Birth to 5 years | Motor development and coordinations |
| Birth to 10 years | First and second language development |
| 1 year to 5 years | Mathematical and logical thinking |
| 3 years to 10 years | Music appreciation and learning |

growth, we are now prepared to look more specifically at the present and emerging capabilities of the newborn.

## The Neonate

**neonatal period:**
the first four weeks of extrauterine life

The **neonatal period** is usually defined as the first four weeks of life and is a critical period in infant development. Many physiological adjustments required for extrauterine existence are taking place. During this period, all bodily functions and psychological states are monitored to ensure a healthy beginning.

**vernix caseosa:**
the oily covering that protects the skin of the fetus

Physically, the newborn may be a frightful sight, though the infant's parents may disagree with this generalization. The skin is wrinkled, red, and covered with a cheeselike, greasy substance called **vernix caseosa,** which protects the skin during uterine development. In addition, the head is large in proportion to the rest of the body; the chest circumference is smaller than that of the infant's head. Sometimes, the neonate's head has become temporarily misshapen during a lengthy delivery. Following the struggle to enter the world, some infants fall into a deep sleep and for the first day or so may even have difficulty staying awake long enough to nurse.

**reflex:**
an unlearned, involuntary response to stimuli

**subcortical:**
the portion of the brain just below the cerebral cortex that is responsible for controlling unlearned and reflexive behavior.

## Reflexes

**cerebral cortex:**
the outer layer of the cerebral hemisphere made that is mostly responsible for higher mental functions, sensory processing, and motor control

The full-term neonate is quite prepared for life and is equipped with a number of inborn movement patterns that help it adapt to new surroundings and new demands. These movement patterns, many of which are present prior to birth, are reflexes. **Reflexes** are unlearned, automatic responses to stimuli resulting from earliest neuromuscular development. Both Jeremy and Angela display the infant rooting and sucking reflexes. For the most part, these early reflexes are a function of **subcortical** (brain stem and spinal cord) mechanisms, though some cortical control is evident. The **cerebral cortex** is the part of the brain that is responsible for perception, memory, and thinking. Figure 5.4 illustrates the regions of the brain and their respective responsibilities.

**survival reflex:**
reflexes that are essential to sustaining life

Some reflexes are called **survival reflexes** because they are necessary for the infant to sustain life. The obvious example is breathing. The birth cry, which sometimes occurs before the infant is fully delivered, sets the respiratory mech-

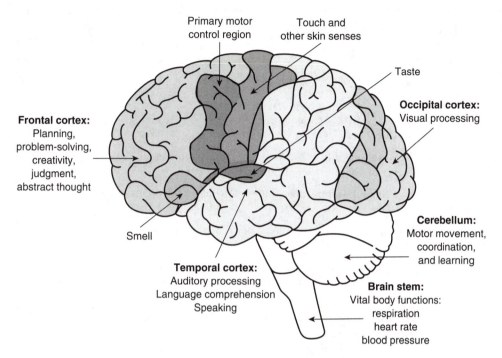

**FIGURE 5.4**
Regions of the Brain and Their Functions

anisms in motion, oxygenating the red blood cells and expelling carbon dioxide from the lungs. Gagging, sneezing, and hiccuping reflexes are present before and after birth.

Most subcortical or **primitive reflexes** gradually disappear as the cerebral cortex matures and begins to direct and control bodily movements and behaviors. Some reflexes such as breathing and other involuntary functions, such as bladder and bowel control, may continue to have elements of both subcortical and cortical control. The developmental course of the individual reflexes varies; some disappear in the first few days, others vanish within the first 12–18 months, and still others persist throughout life, becoming more precise and organized.

In preterm infants, subcortical reflexes are frequently not evident at birth but will appear soon thereafter. Premature infants often exhibit weak rooting and sucking responses. Continued absence or weakness of these early reflexes suggests delayed development or dysfunction in the central nervous system. In premature infants, these early reflexes disappear somewhat more slowly than they do in full-term infants. Table 5.2 lists some major reflexes observed in early infancy.

In addition to an impressive array of reflexes, there are other early behaviors of special interest. They are infant psychological states and activity levels, sensory capabilities, and expected growth and development patterns.

**primitive reflex:** reflexes, controlled by subcortical structures in the brain, that gradually disappear during the first year

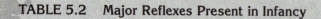

## TABLE 5.2    Major Reflexes Present in Infancy

| Reflex | Description |
| --- | --- |
| **Survival Reflexes** | |
| Breathing reflex | Inhales/exhales, oxygenating the red blood cells and expelling carbon dioxide. |
| Rooting reflex | Turns in direction of touch on the cheek as though searching for a nipple. Serves to orient the infant to breast or bottle. |
| Sucking and swallowing reflex | Stimulated by nipple placed in mouth; allows the infant to take in nourishment. |
| Eyeblink and pupillary reflex | Eyes close or blink; pupils dilate or constrict to protect the eyes. |
| **Primitive Reflexes** | |
| Grasping reflex | Holds firmly to an object touching the palm of the hand. Disappearance around the fourth month signals advancing neurological development. |
| Moro reflex | Often referred to as the *startle reflex;* a loud noise or sudden jolt will cause the arms to thrust outward, then return to an embrace-like position. Disappearance around the fifth or sixth month signals advancing neurological development. |
| Babinski reflex | Toes fan outward, then curl when the bottom of the foot is stroked. Disappearance by end of first year signals advancing neurological development. |
| Tonic neck reflex | A "fencing pose," often assumed when sleeping—head turned to one side, arm extended on the same side, and opposite arm and leg flexed at the elbow and knee. Disappearance around 7 months signals advancing neurological development. |

## Psychological States, Temperament, and Activity Levels

*Jeremy,* now 48 hours old, is cradled in his mother's arms and sleeping quite soundly. His face is scrunched into a tight expression—eyes tightly closed, mouth puckered into an overbite position, chin almost buried in his chest. He is swaddled snugly under the soft baby wrap, arms folded comfortably against his chest, knees bent slightly upward, and toes pointed inward.

Ann attempts to rouse her sleeping baby by gently rubbing her fingers across his soft cheek. He squirms slightly, stretching his legs and turning his head toward the touch; his mouth opens slightly, but he resists waking and returns to his previous comfortable sleeping state. His mouth makes faint sucking movements briefly before he lapses into a fairly deep sleep.

*Angela,* now two weeks old and home from the neonatal care unit, is crying vigorously. Her legs stretch stiffly, and her arms and hands flail in the air. Her blanket is in disarray, and her mother is hurriedly preparing a bottle to feed her. As the nipple of the bottle brushes against her lips, Angela frantically and clumsily searches and struggles to grasp it. Her sucking response is somewhat weak,

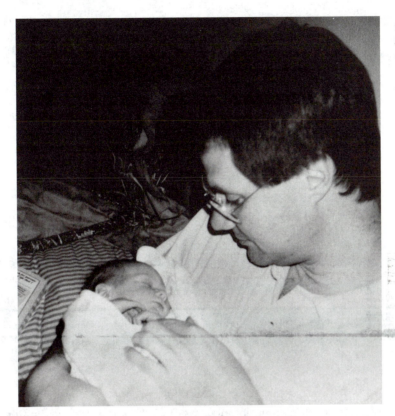

*Babies exhibit great variation in both amount and types of sleep behavior.*

and she whimpers until she succeeds in securing the nipple and the hunger pains begin to subside. The warmth and comfort of nourishment calm and soothe her.

Psychologists use the term **psychological state** when describing the infant's relationship to the outside world. States are characterized in terms of the degree of arousal and alertness the infant exhibits.

**psychological state:** pertains to conditions of arousal and alertness in infancy

*Sleep Behavior.*   An eagerly awaited milestone in infant development is the ability to sleep through the night. Sleeping patterns of infants are often the subject of conversation with proud (or tired) parents. Researchers also are interested in infant sleep patterns. Patterns, characteristics, and problems of sleep in young children make up a large body of literature and a broad field of study.

Sleep patterns change as infants mature. Newborn infants usually sleep approximately 18 out of 24 hours (Berg, Adkinson, & Strock, 1973). The longest period of sleep may be 4 to 4½ hours during the first days. By four to six weeks of age, the infant may be sleeping 12 to 14 hours a day, taking as many as seven "naps" during a 24-hour period.

Some infants sleep a six-hour night by the fourth week after birth, but some will not sleep through the night until they are seven or eight months old. Some infants sleep more during the day and others sleep more at night, though most infants seem to sleep for longer periods at night. There is great variation in both

---

**TABLE 5.3    Classification of Infant States**

| State | Characteristics |
|---|---|
| Regular sleep | Little body movement; regular breathing; no response to mild stimulation. |
| Irregular sleep | Increased body movements; irregular breathing; more easily aroused by external stimuli. |
| Periodic sleep | Occurs between regular and irregular sleep and is accompanied by muscle movements and rapid breathing, then short periods of calm inactivity. |
| Drowsiness | Little motor activity, yet sensitive to external stimuli. |
| Alert inactivity | Visually and/or auditorially scans the environment; large motor activity (head, trunk, arms and legs), alert and relaxed. |
| Waking activity | More intense motor activity may signal physiological need. |
| Crying | Motor activity passes into a whimpering, crying state, becoming louder as distress increases. Thrashing; twisting of torso and kicking vigorously. |

*Source:* Reprinted from *Psychological Issues,* "Causes, Controls and Organization of Behavior in the Neonate" by P. H. Wolff. By permission of International Universities Press, Inc. Copyright © 1966 by International Universities Press.

the amount and type of sleep exhibited in infancy. In his now well-known study of states of arousal in infancy, Wolff (1966) identified six states, summarized in Table 5.3.

By observing eye movements beneath the eyelid during sleep, the infant's sleep phase can be determined. There are two sleep phases, *rapid eye movement (REM)* and *non-rapid eye movement (NREM)* sleep. REM sleep is characterized by closed eyes; uneven respiration; limp muscle tone; intermittent smiles, grimaces, sighs, and sucking movements; and rapid eye movement beneath the eyelids as though the infant is dreaming. NREM sleep ranges from eyes partially open or still closed and a very light activity level with mild startles, to alertness but minimal motor activity, to eyes open with increased motor activity and reactions to external stimuli, to crying, sometimes quite intense.

Sleep researchers believe that REM sleep is vital to growth of the central nervous system. Observations of infant sleep states and patterns help physicians to identify central nervous system abnormalities. For instance, preterm infants generally display a greater amount of REM sleep. There is some evidence that infants suffering from brain injury or birth trauma may exhibit disturbed REM/NREM sleep patterns.

*Jeremy,* now four months old, is usually quite content at bedtime. His mother usually holds him in her lap for awhile after the evening feeding, while he drifts into drowsiness and then into irregular sleep. Her soft voice hums to him while he languishes in her arms. Sensing his readiness for the crib, she carries him to his room. Placing him quietly in his crib, she continues to hum. She rubs his back softly and then leaves the room after observing that he will soon fall soundly to sleep.

However, on this particular evening, Jeremy resists sleep. His eyes are open and scanning his surroundings, though he appears tired and cries sporadically. Tonight, he is what most parents would call "cranky." His mother, also tired, wishes that some magic formula would soothe him and help him to rest. Nevertheless, after determining that Jeremy is not hungry, his diaper does not need changing, and his clothing is comfortable, she follows her established routine with him, sustaining each phase slightly longer. After being placed in his crib, he rouses somewhat and cries resistively while Ann strokes his back gently. Though he has not fallen into sound sleep, she leaves the room.

Predictable, unhurried bedtimes with regular routines help the reluctant infant to separate from the family and fall asleep more readily. Routines may include a relaxed bathtime during which the interaction between parent and child is enjoyable, followed by being held in the parent's lap, rocked, and sung to softly. Cuddling a soft stuffed toy while being held focuses attention away from more stimulating activities occurring around the infant. This routine is followed by being placed in bed with a moment of slow back rubbing and a kiss on the cheek, a spoken "good night," and then departure from the room.

A study of night waking among nine-month-old infants found that infants whose parent or caregiver routinely remained present with them at bedtime until they fell asleep were more likely to wake during the night (Adair, Baucher, Philipp, Levenson, & Zuckerman, 1991). This finding suggests that putting infants to bed when they are at least partially awake elicits their own internal devices for falling asleep. If the infant wakes during the night, barring problems such as hunger, discomfort, or impending illness, he or she can learn to employ the same internal devices rather than soliciting parental assistance. While this study did not establish actual cause and effect, the researchers suggested that infant temperament may be a factor, but parental difficulty in separating from the infant may also interfere with infant sustained sleep patterns. Other reasons for night waking include being too cold or too warm and needing appropriate clothing or bed covers, colic, an unfamiliar bed or new surroundings, disturbing sensory stimuli such as loud or startling noises, and distracting lights. Some infants signal that they are awake; others do not unless they are in some form of distress such as hunger or uncomfortable clothing. Infants generally sleep through the night by age three months, typically from five to eight hours.

Sleep routines vary from family to family and in child care settings, and though sleep patterns are enhanced by predictable and reassuring rituals, the household need not be abnormally quiet, as infants generally adjust to reasonable and typical noises in their environments. Nor should siblings be expected to be particularly quiet—though rowdy play, of course, disturbs anyone's rest. Some infants may actually be soothed by usual household noises, which often provide an auditory sense of the permanence of people and the predictability of routines.

Similar routines in out-of-home child care arrangements facilitate naptime for infants and reassure them of the support of their caregivers. As with noise levels at home, rest times away from home can be scheduled during periods of the day when noise levels are at a minimum; yet there is no need to expect that all noise can be curtailed during group care naptimes.

**temperament:** an individual's behavior style that is both biologically and environmentally derived

*Temperament.*   **Temperament** is an individual's biologically based behavior style that helps us to describe the infant's responses (Chess, 1967; Thomas & Chess, 1977; Thomas, Chess, & Birch, 1968). This aspect of infant development will be discussed more fully in Chapter 6; it is mentioned here as one of the psychological states in infancy. Chess and Thomas (1987) identified several dimensions of temperament, including activity level, rhythms, approach and withdrawal behaviors, adaptability, responsiveness, intensity of reaction, quality of mood, distractability, and attention span and persistence. Using these activity classifications, the researchers delineated three basic temperament patterns: *easy, difficult,* and *slow to warm up.* These behavior styles influence the reciprocal interactions between infants and their caregivers. There are wide variations in temperaments among infants. Some infants are less able to calm themselves than others; some are easily comforted by their caregivers.

*Angela* is less easily soothed than Jeremy. At bedtime, she is quite fretful and restless. Inferring from the usual afternoon and evening family routines that bedtime is drawing near, she begins to whimper and cry and will not sustain her grasp on a soft toy offered to her. She resists being held or comforted.

Since birth, Angela has had a variety of caregivers, from hospital neonatal care nursing staff in her first two weeks to a home with extended family, including her grandmother and her own mother's siblings—some young children and some teenagers. Each has taken turns caring for and feeding her. Thus, Angela's care has been neither predictable nor consistent.

Angela's grandmother, sensing a difficult bedtime, intervenes. She carries Angela on her shoulder as she walks around the house giving cleanup and bedtime instructions to the other children. Patting a fretful Angela, she continues to walk, talk, and hush the baby. When this proves unsuccessful, she proceeds to a back bedroom, where, separated from the rest of the family, she places Angela across her lap and begins to sing and talk softly to her. For a time, Angela still wiggles, lifts her head and frets, and is easily distracted by the sound of children playing inside the house. Her grandmother continues to sing and talk or hum until at last Angela begins to rest and finally dozes.

Temperament is readily observable in infancy, expressing itself through various behaviors such as the ability to cope with stress, delay gratification, or modulate emotions. In the preceding vignette, Angela seems unable to deal with the distractions around her and to self-calm, and she becomes more agitated as others try to comfort her.

While individual styles of behaving endure over time, the behavior itself is expressed in age-related forms. For instance, Angela's resistance to adult efforts to comfort may at a later age emerge into self-comforting strategies such as thumb-sucking, singing or talking to herself, or seeking a certain person, place, chair, pillow, or blanket that is associated with calmness and rest.

The activity levels of neonates have been positively correlated with activity levels at ages four and eight (Korner et al., 1985). Activity levels have also been associated with birth order (Eaton, Chipperfield, & Singbell, 1989). A study of 7,000 children ranging in age from four days to seven years, including first- through sixth-born children, found that earlier-born children were more active than later-born children. Heredity seems to play a role in determining individual temperament, as does a child's environment. However, the relative influence of each has not been established.

## Sensory Capabilities in Infancy

During the prenatal period, neurological development emerges intrinsically as a result of the properly timed activation of genes that are not dependent on external input or neural activity (Delcomyn, 1998). However, during later prenatal development and the early months and years of infancy and early childhood, external input is critical to normal development. Environmental input stimulates electrical activity in neurons, resulting in the process of circuitry building, or "wiring," of the neurological system as nerve cells grow axons and dendrites that navigate toward their targets, forming important connections for the relay of messages throughout the body. The fact that the nervous system can be shaped by neural activity aroused by environmental stimuli is evidence of the brain's **plasticity,** which is most apparent when neuron connections are forming. This means that an individual's brain has the remarkable ability to change and compensate for problems if intervention is timely and intensive. However, inappropriate or negative experiences as with child abuse and neglect, have been found to interfere with normal wiring of the brain resulting in adverse developmental outcomes (Chugani, 1997; Perry, 1993a, 1993b). These early environmental stimuli have important implications for the development and integrity of the sensory and motor systems.

**plasticity:**
the ability of the brain to rewire itself as when repeated experiences (good or bad) result in divergent connections between neurons

The newborn's sensory equipment is remarkably operative at birth. Neonates are capable of seeing, hearing, tasting, smelling, and responding to touch. The neonate takes in and processes information to a much greater extent than we might expect. **Perceptual** development begins as the infant seeks and receives information through the senses.

**perceptual:**
the physiological process by which sensory input is interpreted

*Touch.*   Scientists believe the sense of touch emerges between 7½ and 14 weeks of embryonic development (Hooker, 1952). Skin, muscular, and inner ear (vestibular) senses are more mature at birth than are the other senses (Gottfried, 1984). The sense of touch, particularly around the mouth area, is especially acute and facilitates infant rooting and nursing. Certain other parts of the body are sensitive to touch. These include the nose, skin of the forehead, soles of the feet, and genitals. Most of the reflexes listed in Table 5.1 are stimulated by touch. In addition to touch, the skin is sensitive to temperature, pressure, and pain.

For obvious ethical reasons, little research exists on sensitivity to pain. Contrary to the previous notion that neonates do not experience great pain, we now know they do. Recent studies of pain associated with infant circumcision procedures have helped to advance knowledge about infant pain. By analyzing the recorded vocalizations of newborn males during circumcision, researchers identified significant differences in vocalizations as each step of the procedure became more invasive (Porter, Miller, & Marshall, 1986). Some surgical procedures that were previously thought to be painless for newborns are now accompanied by analgesia or anesthesia whenever possible (American Academy of Family Physicians, 1996; American Academy of Pediatrics and American College of Obstetricians and Gynecologists, 1992; Ryan & Finer, 1994). Recognizing that infants do indeed experience pain with various medical

*Infants enjoy and benefit from visually interesting baby books and pictures.*

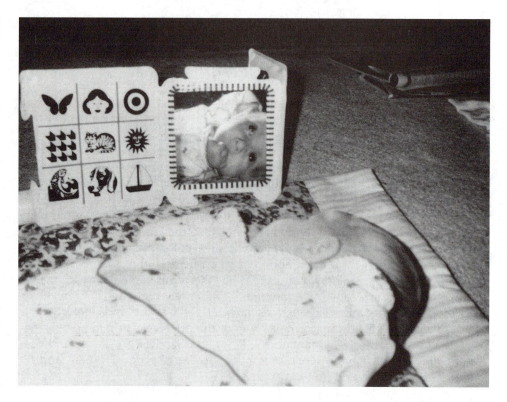

procedures, research continues to identify safe methods for reducing pain. For instance, it has been found that giving newborns a drink of a sucrose solution moments before the routine heel prick to test a blood sample for the presence of PKU appears to reduce the pain of the procedure (Blass & Shah, 1995).

Studies of preterm infants have found that touch plays a very significant role in their development. Many neonatal care units encourage parents of preterm infants in particular to gently hold and caress them (when the infant's physical condition permits). When the infant cannot be held, gently caressing the infant in the isolette is encouraged. In some hospitals, volunteers hold, rock, and softly stroke these small and vulnerable babies. A study by T. M. Field and her colleagues (1986) found that preterm infants who were gently touched and caressed several times each day gained weight faster than preterm infants who did not receive this regular stimulation. These infants also exhibited advanced mental and motor development at the end of the first year compared to the control group infants.

The importance of touch and the infant's need for it have been of interest to researchers for years. Lack of soothing tactile sensations during infancy has been associated with delays in cognitive and affective development (Ainsworth, 1962; Yarrow, 1961). Thus, in addition to the sheer pleasure experienced by both infant and caregiver that hugging, rocking, caressing, and patting bring, these experiences provide the infant with the tactile stimulation that is essential to perceptual and sensory development.

*Vision.*     The neonate's vision functions well at birth, though visual acuity is imperfect, with a tendency toward nearsightedness (Cornell & McDonnell,

1986). Neonates can follow a moving light and fixate on an object at a distance of about 9 inches. In his pioneering studies of infant visual preferences, Fantz (1961) found that infants prefer human faces, enjoy bold patterns such as checkerboards or bull's-eye patterns, and tend to look at the edges of the designs or at the point where two contrasts come together. While bold patterns appear to hold the infant's attention, research has demonstrated that infants demonstrate interest through fixed gazes in color, showing a preference for blue and green objects over red ones (R. J. Adams, Mauer, & Davis, 1986). Bornstein (1984, 1985) also found that infants respond to differences in colors and suggested that later ability to categorize by color, thought to be a result of cognitive development, has its origins in the earliest visual perceptual processes. Other researchers have found that infants watch more intently a face that is active, smiling, talking, blinking, or laughing (Haith, 1966; Samuels, 1985). Others have found that infants attend longer to a face that imitates their own facial movements and expressions (Winnicott, 1971). Whereas vision improves rapidly over the first few months of life, mature 20/20 vision is not achieved until about age five (Bornstein, 1988).

*Hearing.*   Though the passages of the ear (eustachian tubes and external canal) may still contain amniotic fluids for the first few days after birth, the newborn hears fairly well. After the fluids are absorbed, the neonate responds vigorously to various sounds in the environment. The infant is startled by loud noises and soothed by soft sounds. It has been suggested that neonates can discriminate between loud and soft sounds but do not respond to variations in pitch (Bench, 1978). Researchers have also demonstrated that neonates are capable of discriminating among sounds that differ in duration, direction, and frequency as well as loudness (Bower, 1982).

Neonates seem particularly responsive to the human voice (Caron, Caron, & MacLean, 1988). The neonate will often stop crying when spoken to, visually scan for the source of the voice, and attempt to vocalize (Rosenthal, 1982). Could it be that human infants are genetically "programmed" to react to human speech?

It has been estimated that about 1 in 1,000 otherwise well infants have bilateral (both sides) congenital hearing loss, and among infants in neonatal intensive care, the incidence was found to be 5 in 1,000 (Mason & Herrmann, 1998). Because hearing loss in infants if left undetected and untreated can lead to speech and language delays, learning difficulties, and social and emotional problems, the medical profession now makes every effort to screen infants before they are six months old. In 1993, the National Institutes of Health recommended that all infants receive hearing screening within the first three months of life (National Institutes of Health, 1993). Success of intervention strategies depends upon earliest possible detection.

*Taste.*   Newborns are very responsive to variations in taste. The taste of milk seems to elicit a reaction of satisfaction in infants. Infants prefer sweet tastes and usually react negatively to sour, bitter, or salty tastes (Steiner, 1979).

*Smell.*   Infants sense a variety of odors and will turn away from noxious odors such as vinegar or alcohol. Interestingly, they seem able to recognize the smell of their mothers within the first few days of life (MacFarlane, 1977; Makin &

Porter, 1989) and will turn away from an unused breast pad or the breast pad of another mother. Musick and Householder (1986) suggest that the early bonding process might be facilitated if the mother left her breast pad or another small article of her clothing in the bassinet to reinforce the infant's sensory attachment to her.

## PHYSICAL AND MOTOR DEVELOPMENT DURING THE FIRST YEAR

Growth and development during this first year are both dramatic and significant. According to Sandra Anselmo, "In no other one-year period until puberty are there so many physical changes. The changes in infancy are measured in terms of days and weeks rather than in terms of months and years" (1987, p. 148).

### Physical Characteristics

Birth weight and birth length are always of interest to parents, grandparents, and health care professionals. While birth weight and birth length often make for proud conversation, physical measurements are quite significant in the context of infant health and development. Low birth weight, for instance, has serious implications for survival and for subsequent normal development.

The average birth weight for full-term infants is 7½ pounds, with a range from 5½ to 10 pounds. Boys usually are slightly heavier than girls at birth. Birth length ranges from 18 to 22 inches, with an average of 20 inches. The neonate frequently loses weight in the first few days because of loss of body fluids and the inability to adequately take in nourishment but will gain at a rate of 6 to 8 ounces per week and by five to six months may have doubled the birth weight. The infant's length also will have increased, by 6 to 7 inches.

During the second half of the first year, gains in pounds and inches decelerate somewhat, though growth continues at a rapid pace. Weight may increase by 4 to 6 ounces weekly and height by 3 to 4 inches. By the first birthday, infants may have tripled in weight and grown 10 to 12 inches since birth. If growth were to proceed at such pace, an 18-year-old would measure more than 15 feet tall and weigh several tons! Fortunately, growth slows appreciably after the first two years.

Weight and height are observable characteristics. While this outward growth is readily observable, significant internal growth is taking place as the central nervous system matures and bones and muscles increase in weight, length, and coordination.

**ossify:**
to convert cartilage or membrane to bone

The soft bones of early infancy gradually **ossify** as calcium and other minerals harden them. The bones are soft and pliable and are difficult to break. They do not support the infant's weight in sitting or standing positions. The skull bones are separated by **fontanelles** (often called "soft spots"), which may compress to facilitate passage through the birth canal. These fontanelles tend to shrink after six months and may close between 9 and 18 months.

**fontanelles:**
membranous space between the cranial bones of the fetus and infant

Interestingly, the bones of the skull and wrists ossify earliest, the wrists and ankles developing more bones as the child matures. Girls may be several weeks ahead of boys in bone development at birth. Physicians may use X-rays of the wrists to determine the **skeletal age** of individual children. Such X-rays reveal

**skeletal age:**
a measure of physical development based on examination of skeletal X-rays

the number of bones in the wrist along with the extent of ossification. This information assists in assessing expected growth progress and diagnosing growth disorders and disease.

Though infants are born with all the muscle cells they will ever have (Tanner, 1989), there is a large amount of water in muscle tissue. Gradually, as protein and other nutrients replace this cellular fluid, the strength of the muscles increases.

Since neurological development and brain growth are rapid during prenatal development and the first year, head circumference measures provide a useful means for evaluating the status of the central nervous system in infants and young children. Small-for-age head circumference measurements at eight months to two years of age may indicate central nervous system anomalies that are associated with developmental delay. As is true of other organs, not all parts of the brain develop at the same rate. At birth, the brain stem and the midbrain are the most highly developed. These areas of the brain control consciousness, inborn reflexes, digestion, respiration, and elimination.

The cerebrum and the cerebral cortex surround the midbrain and are significant in the development of primary motor and sensory responses. Following the law of developmental direction, the nerve cells that control the upper trunk and arms mature before those that control the lower trunk and legs. Observation of infant motor activity reveals a growing number of skills that use the muscles of the neck, arms, and hands, skills that precede the abilities to turn over, sit up, or crawl. By six months of age, the cerebral cortex has matured sufficiently to control most of the infant's physical activity. At this point in growth and development, many of the reflexes of early infancy should be fading, signaling maturation of the neurological system.

## Expected Patterns and Developmental Milestones

Recall the examples at the beginning of the chapter drawn from cross-cultural studies of variations in child growth and development. Both timing and sequence of development can vary among and within cultures and racial groups. As we described earlier in this chapter, current thinking about expected patterns of growth and development calls for a consideration of geographic, cultural, and socioeconomic factors that facilitate (or in some cases impede) growth and development. Parental goals and expectations influence growth and development through the types and timing of educational or enrichment opportunities that they provide, the quality and quantity of play that is encouraged, and the behaviors that they elicit through their interactions with their children (Bronfenbrenner, 1986; Garrett et al., 1994; Ogbu, 1981). Therefore, in studying Table 5.4, consider the ages as approximations and recognize that the sequence may indeed vary. For instance, some children scoot in a seated position rather than crawl. This represents a variation, but not a developmental abnormality.

## Relationship of Physical and Motor Development to Psychosocial Development

Increasing physical and motor abilities during the first year expand the infant's psychosocial horizons. By communicating hunger, pain, and happiness cues

## TABLE 5.4    Developmental Milestones in Motor Control during the First Year

| Age | Motor Development |
|---|---|
| Birth to 3 months | Supports head when in prone position |
| | Lifts head |
| | Supports weight on elbows |
| | Hands relax from the grasping reflex |
| | Visually follows a moving object |
| | Pushes with feet against lap when held upright |
| | Makes reflexive stepping movements when held in a standing position |
| | Sits with support |
| | Turns from side to back |
| 3 to 6 months | Slaps at bath water |
| | Kicks feet when prone |
| | Plays with toes |
| | Reaches but misses dangling object |
| | Shakes and stares at toy placed in hand |
| | Head self-supported when held at shoulder |
| | Turns from back to side |
| | Sits with props |
| | Makes effort to sit alone |
| | Exhibits crawling behaviors |
| | Rocks on all fours |
| | Draws knees up and falls forward |
| 6 to 9 months | Rolls from back to stomach |
| | Crawls using both hands and feet |
| | Sits alone steadily |
| | Pulls to standing position in crib |
| | Raises self to sitting posture |
| | Successfully reaches and grasps toy |
| | Transfers object from one hand to the other |
| | Stands up by furniture |
| | Cruises along crib rail |
| | Makes stepping movements around furniture |
| 9 to 12 months | Exhibits "mature" crawling |
| | Cruises holding on to furniture |
| | Walks with two hands held |
| | Sits without falling |
| | Stands alone |
| | May walk alone |
| | Attempts to crawl up stairs |
| | Grasps object with thumb and forefinger |

*As a rule, motor development proceeds from the upper regions of the body to the lower.*

through crying, cooing, and other vocalizations, infants learn that they can draw others into interactions with them. When these interactions are positive and supportive, infants learn to trust both parents and caregivers and themselves to meet their needs. Each new developmental milestone brings with it new sets of behaviors and new types of interactions between infant and caregivers. For most infants, each new ability elicits encouragement, praise, and joy, supporting an emerging sense of self. As motor abilities increase, parents, siblings, and caregivers often begin to perceive the infant as more "grown up" and may unwittingly attribute greater self-sufficiency to the infant than is really the case. Misattributions—for example, expecting the infant to hold her own bottle for feeding, judge depth of a stair step, manage playthings designed for older children, and so on—compromise the infant's safety and deflates an emerging sense of confidence.

As the infant becomes more mobile, safety becomes a real and immediate concern. Concerns about safety bring about new forms of communicating that include facial expressions, voice tone and pitch, and verbal cautions and commands. Keeping children safe while encouraging the types of activities that enhance motor development requires both vigilance and understanding. Undue restraint and excessive restrictions, particularly if delivered in impatience and anger, frighten and confuse the infant. Such interactions can reduce children's emerging self-confidence and willingness to explore, learn, and express themselves (Comer & Poussant, 1992). While it may be necessary to say "no" and "don't touch" often, overuse of such restrictions can cause infants to associate negative and disapproving responses with the people who mean the most to them. Attempts to explore and investigate and to try out emerging skills are thus hindered as is the confidence and independence that new skills bring. It is better to establish safe, "child-friendly" environments with supervision that offers substitutes and distractions than to impose constant verbal restrictions (Meyerhoff, 1994).

## Relationship of Physical and Motor Development to Cognition

Motor experiences in infancy form the basis of meaning in earliest cognitive development. At first, movements are unintentional (as with many reflexes); later, most of them become purposeful. Piaget's (1952) stages of cognitive development begin with the *sensorimotor* stage, from birth to age two. This sensorimotor stage of cognitive development follows a pattern from random, involuntary reflex activity, in which cognition is dominated by sensory input, to anticipatory and intentional behaviors that are facilitated by increasing large and fine motor controls and mobility.

An environment that is rich in sensory input—sights, sounds, tastes, aromas, textures, and movement—has been shown to enhance brain growth and neurological development in infants (Shore, 1997). Talking, singing, sharing books, and interacting socially with the infant provide needed input for a rapidly developing mind. An environment that encourages social interactions and freedom to explore is essential to a well-integrated neurological and cognitive system.

## FACTORS INFLUENCING PHYSICAL AND MOTOR DEVELOPMENT

### Genetic Makeup

Each infant is a unique individual with a special genetic endowment. This genetic endowment is observable in physical features such as eye, hair, and skin color; shape and size of facial features; body build; activity levels; and so on. It is also related to mental and psychosocial characteristics such as temperament, some forms of mental retardation, and certain psychological disorders. Contemporary research in genetics is beginning to pinpoint the influence of heredity on less observable characteristics such as size and functioning of the internal organs, susceptibility to disease, psychological strengths and disorders, and numerous other facets of human individuality. Contemporary gene mapping research holds promise for identifying genetic anomalies and perhaps gene therapy to alleviate or minimize the influence of certain genes on developmental outcomes. Screening tests during pregnancy to detect genetic abnormalities allow for early identification and consideration of appropriate intervention strategies.

### Integrity of Prenatal Development

Chapter 3 described very rapid development during the prenatal period. To the extent that this critical period in growth and development is protected from hazard, the integrity of the fetus is ensured. Studies of the vulnerability of the fetus during various prenatal stages indicate that there are both immediate and long-term effects of unhealthy intrauterine environments (Bornstein & Lamb, 1992). Infants who benefit from a healthy prenatal journey—one that is free of drugs, toxins, poor nutrition, maternal stress, and other environmental hazards—are less likely to experience the myriad and sometimes devastating health, growth, and developmental outcomes associated with poor or inadequate intrauterine environments.

## Preterm and Low-Birth-Weight Infants

Prematurity is measured by *gestational age,* which ranges from 23 weeks or less to a full term of 38–42 weeks. Gestational age is an important predictor of survival and developmental outcomes. Infants born at full term but weighing less than expected for a full-term baby are considered *small for gestational age (SGA).* Usually, these infants are healthy, but they are immature and small and have insufficient body fat to assist in regulation of body temperature. Weight gain is usually their primary challenge; however, there may be other, more serious reasons for the infant's failure to gain sufficient weight in utero. Low-birth-weight (LBW) infants range from 3.5 to 5.5 pounds. Infants in this birth weight range not only must build fat stores but, perhaps more critical, may face respiratory distress syndrome (RDS) because of immature lungs and breathing mechanisms. While the majority of LBW infants have normal outcomes, they are at higher risk for mild to severe problems in cognition, cerebral palsy, convulsions, delayed speech, and visual and auditory impairments.

Very low-birth-weight (VLBW) infants weigh less than 3 pounds. These infants are extremely immature and need intensive neonatal care to help them survive. VLBW infants account for only 1.2 percent of births, however, these infants account for 46 percent of infant deaths (National Center for Health Statistics, 1994). They are at higher risk of dying in the first 28 days—some estimate 40 times more likely—than mature newborns (Brecht, 1989). Sometimes, their care requires lengthy and costly hospitalization. While advances in neonatal medicine have resulted in increased survival prospects for these tiny babies, they are at extreme risk for long-term health problems and disabilities (see Table 5.5).

Preventing prematurity and low birth weight in neonates is a complex and challenging task that involves addressing a number of issues: poverty, at-risk lifestyles, poor nutrition, inadequate health care, age, number, and character of prior pregnancies, genetics, in utero medical treatment, modern medical discoveries, ethics, and education.

## GENERAL HEALTH AND FREEDOM FROM DISEASE

### Regular Health Checkups and Immunizations

Regular visits to the pediatrician or family health care specialist are necessary to monitor the infant's progress in growth and development, assess nutritional needs, treat infections, allergies, and illness, and administer disease-preventing immunizations. The American Academy of Pediatrics recommends preventive health care visits for healthy infants and children at 1, 2, 4, 6, 9, 12, 15, and 18 months, then annually from ages two through six, and then every two years through adolescence. More frequent visits may be necessary for children with special needs and between regular checkups as the need arises. Newborns are routinely tested for phenylketonuria (PKU), an inborn error of metabolism in which abnormal levels of the enzyme phenylalanine form in the blood that, if untreated, leads to mental retardation and other abnormalities. When detected and treated within the first three weeks after birth with a specialized diet, developmental outcomes are better than when the diet is started later. In addition to

### TABLE 5.5   When to Worry about At-Risk Infants and Toddlers

| Age | Phase | Primary Tasks | Warning Signs |
|---|---|---|---|
| 0–3 months | Taking In | Crying for basic needs, developing attention, calming when needs met | Poor head control, no social smile, no visual/auditory responses, feeding problems, difficult to soothe, not attentive to faces |
| 4–8 months | Reaching Out | Attachment to adult, expanding interest in toys and people | No sitting, no mobility, no vocalizations, not seeking attention, not interested in toys/objects, feeding and sleeping problems |
| 9–14 months | Moving Out | Exploration, communication | Not moving from one position to another, asymmetric movement, no imitation, rigid play routines, no gestural or verbal communication |
| 14–20 months | Speaking Up | Learning by imitation, seeking independence | Not walking, not talking, not understanding directions, not using objects for intended purposes |
| 21–30 months | Speaking Out | Imagination, communication | Few words, no word combinations, no constructive or imaginative play, persistent withdrawn or aggressive behaviors |
| 30–42 months | Play Alone | Independence, peer relations | Does not attend to age-appropriate tasks to completion, withdrawn or repetitive behaviors that cannot be interrupted, unintelligible speech, tantrums, lack of independence in self-help skills |

*Source:* Andrew C. (1998). When to worry about infants and toddlers 'at risk.' *ACEI Focus on Infants and Toddlers, 11,* p. 2. With permission of the Association for Childhood Education International.

checking growth progress through weight, height, and head circumference measurements, the physician and parent have an opportunity to discuss the child's growth and development, preventive health care measures, individual nutritional requirements, treatment of allergies, and other health and developmental concerns.

Fortunately, immunizations now prevent many life-threatening diseases in infants and children, and many promising new vaccines are on the horizon. Infants and young children receive a standard series of immunizations against hepatitis B, diphtheria, tetanus, pertussis (whooping cough), *H. influenza* type B, polio, measles, mumps, and rubella. All of these immunizations need to be given to children before they are two years old to protect them during their most vulnerable early months and years. Recommended vaccination schedules are updated annually and published every January. The American Academy of Pediatrics, in collaboration with the U.S. Centers for Disease Control and the

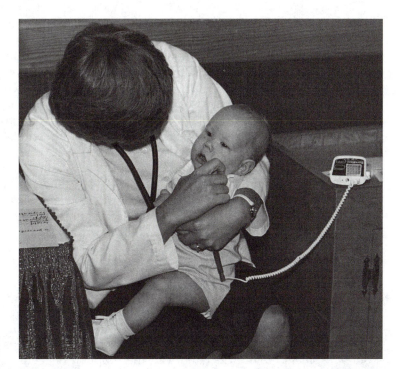

*Preventive health care is provided through regular checkups and immunizations.*

American Association of Family Physicians, develops the schedule and through practices doctors' individual and local health departments advise parents of any revisions or additions to the immunization schedule, as well as the availability of new or improved immunizations and alternative methods for administering them (e.g., nasal spray, skin patches, time-release pills, genetically engineered food products). Additional vaccines are also available and administered when advisable, including chicken pox and rotavirus vaccines. (Rotavirus is a virus that is responsible for the most common cause of diarrhea in infants and young children. Untreated diarrhea is a serious childhood infection that can be life threatening.) On the horizon are many new and improved vaccines including vaccines for ear infections, asthma, strep throat, juvenile diabetes, multiple sclerosis, AIDS, and some forms of cancer. Advances in genetics and immunology research are truly ushering in a new generation of vaccines and disease prevention and treatment practices.

The National Childhood Vaccine Injury Act (42 U.S.C. §300 aa-26) requires that physicians provide to a child's parent or legal representative before vaccination, information about the vaccine that has been published by the Centers for Disease Control and Prevention. The physician or health care professional administering the vaccine must ensure that the person authorizing the vaccine reads and understands the vaccine information materials.

Unfortunately, the availability of life-saving vaccines has not necessarily resulted in all children being immunized. Many unimmunized children are from families who lack the resources and the knowledge to obtain health care for their children (Federal Interagency Forum on Child and Family Statistics, 1999). Cultural and religious belief systems, misinformation, and fear of risks also influence family health care practices and may prevent some parents from availing themselves of medicines and immunizations. Failure to immunize sometimes results in an alarming resurgence of serious communicable diseases that spread among other unimmunized children and adults. For example, in 1983, there were fewer than 1,500 cases of measles in the United States (Centers for Disease Control, 1992). In 1992, this number escalated to nearly 26,500 cases, with 89 measles-related deaths. The alarming increase in cases of mumps, rubella, German measles, whooping cough, and polio prompted a variety of national (and international) education and dissemination campaigns, including the 1993 federal Vaccines for Children Act, which made vaccines available to physicians free of charge for uninsured, Medicaid-covered, and Native American children. This has appreciably decreased the number of unimmunized children in the United States, though an unacceptable number of infants and children remain unimmunized or underimmunized (Federal Interagency Forum on Child and Family Statistics, 1999).

## Dental Health

The first teeth begin to erupt between five and nine months of age. The first teeth to erupt are usually the two lower middle incisors, followed in a few months by the four upper middle incisors. By the end of the first year, most infants have these six teeth. The complete set of 20 teeth does not erupt until around 2½ years. Pain associated with the eruption of teeth varies among infants. Some infants cry, are sleepy and fretful, seem to want to chew something, and drool considerably. Others appear to feel no pain or discomfort and may, to the surprise of their parents, present a "toothed" smile.

Care of teeth during the first year involves relieving the discomfort accompanying eruptions of new teeth and providing adequate proteins and minerals, particularly calcium and fluoride, in the infant's diet. Fluoride is usually available in adequate amounts in community water supplies; in some cases, however, fluoride supplements are prescribed. As children begin to eat more "grown-up" foods, there is a need to limit such foods as cookies, candies, soft drinks, and sweetened dry cereals that are high in refined carbohydrates. Curtailing indiscriminate use of the bottle also protects infant teeth. "Nursing bottle" caries, or decay, occurs when beverages (milk, juices, and sweetened water) are consumed from infant bottles taken to bed or carried about as a constant companion (Nizel, 1977).

## Nutrition

The role of nutrition in ensuring optimal growth and developmental outcomes is paramount during prenatal development and infancy. During this period of very rapid growth, brain growth is particularly dramatic. Studies have linked impaired functioning of the central nervous system to poor nutrition in the early months of life (Dobbing, 1984; Galler, Ramsey, & Solimano, 1984, 1985). Adequate nutrition helps to prevent illnesses and ensures the developmental integrity of the individual.

**colostrum:**
the first fluid secreted by the breasts soon after birth, before true milk is formed

***Breast or Formula Feeding.***   Because of its biochemical composition, breast milk is uniquely suited to the infant's immature digestive system. It provides initial advantages through **colostrum**, the milk that precedes mature breast milk in the first several days after delivery. Colostrum provides immunity to a number of infections when the mother carries the immunities and is rich in the nutrients a newborn needs. Mature breast milk is secreted between the third and sixth day after childbirth and changes over time (as long as breast-feeding takes place) to match the changing needs of the growing infant. Generally, for the first six months, breast milk provides all the fluids and nutrients an infant needs to be healthy. After six months, a pediatrician may prescribe supplements such as fluoride, Vitamin C, and Vitamin D if there is a need for them and may begin the introduction of selected solid foods. Health care professionals are currently encouraging mothers who choose to breast-feed to do so at least during the earliest months up to five to six months, but advise that continuing to breast-feed for 12 months results in more long-term benefits. Continuation beyond 12 months becomes a matter of mutual desirability (American Academy of Pediatrics Work Group on Breastfeeding, 1997; U.S. Department of Health and Human Services, 1990).

Research documenting the benefits of breast-feeding to both infant and mother are compelling (American Academy of Pediatrics Work Group on Breastfeeding, 1997). For the infant the following short- and long-term outcomes have been identified in numerous research studies in the United States, Canada, Europe, and other developed countries:

- Decreased risk for a number of acute and chronic diseases, including diarrhea, lower respiratory infection, otitis media (infection of the middle ear canal), bacterial meningitis, urinary tract infection, and allergies such as eczema, asthma, rhinitis, and food allergies
- Possible protection against sudden infant death syndrome (SIDS), insulin-dependent diabetes mellitus, ulcerative colitis, Crohn's disease, lymphoma, and chronic digestive diseases
- Possible lowering of low-density lipoproteins, or "bad" cholesterol, in an infant's blood
- Improved oral facial development, preventing later poorly aligned teeth and potential for speech impediments (D. W. Davis & Bell, 1991)
- Possible enhancement of cognitive development and visual acuity (Jorgensen, Hernell, Lund, Hilmer, & Michaelsen, 1996)

For mothers, the benefits of breast-feeding are equally impressive:

- Increases in the level of oxytocin (a hormone that facilitates the excretion of milk through the milk ducts), which lessens postpartum bleeding and helps the uterus to return to its regular size and position
- Burning of more calories resulting in earlier return to prepregnancy weight
- Building of bone strength
- Contribution to family planning (child spacing) by suppressing ovulation
- Reduction of the risk of ovarian cancer and, in premenopausal women, the incidence of breast cancer
- Convenience, as the breast milk has been "properly stored," comes already prepared, and is ready to serve at the appropriate temperature. It can be pumped and stored for feedings when mother must be away or when other members of the family wish to participate in feeding the infant. (See Box 5.1, "Mother-Friendly Employers").

## BOX 5.1    Mother-Friendly Employers

Many mothers juggle their parenting responsibilities and working outside the home. Women who return to work and choose to continue breastfeeding their infants benefit from business practices that are mother-friendly. Businesses, as well, benefit through reduced absenteeism, reduced employee turnover, shorter maternity leaves, increased productivity, recruitment incentive, fewer health insurance claims, and a positive image in the community. A number of states have enacted laws or policies that recognize businesses that are mother-friendly. Such policies include:

A workplace atmosphere that supports a woman's choice to breastfeed her infant

Work schedule flexibility that provides timely breaks for lactating mothers to breast-feed their infants or to express breast milk

A private lactation room that is equipped with a sink and a clean, safe water source for hand washing and for rinsing breast pump equipment, comfortable furnishings, an electrical outlet, a phone, and a locking door or an appropriate "reserved" sign

Access to hygienic storage (e.g., refrigerator, ice chest) where breast milk can be kept cool, safe, and free from contamination

A procedure for informing employees of the employer's mother-friendly policy

Mother-friendly businesses may also provide:

Prenatal or postpartum classes on breast-feeding and infant nutrition through their wellness programs

The services of a lactation consultant

Literature and other resources on infant feeding and nutrition

There are certain foods and substances to be avoided if the mother chooses to breast-feed. Some medications can be dangerous for the infant, though some are not. Both prescription and nonprescription drugs should be used only on the advice of a physician. Illicit drugs, alcohol, and caffeine have all been shown to have dangerous adverse effects on the nursing infant. Some foods ingested by the mother may alter the content and character of the milk and may also disagree with the infant's delicate digestion and absorption system. Certainly, smoking while breast-feeding should be avoided, for the effects of secondhand smoke are now well documented. Indeed, secondhand smoke has been shown to increase the incidence of asthma, wheezing, and chronic bronchitits and the risk of SIDS. (American Academy of Pediatrics, 1998; Gergen, Fowler, Maurer, Davis, & Overpeck, 1998).

Few health care professionals today would not encourage breast-feeding. However, some mothers may be unable to breast-feed for various reasons (infant's health status and hospitalization needs, mother's health, medications, disabilities, employment, adoption) or may simply choose not to do so. For some of these mothers and infants, there is the option to provide human milk provided by human milk donor banks, wherein human milk is obtained from well-screened donors, pasteurized, and made available to eligible applicants. There are six regional human milk banks in North America, five of which are members of the Human Milk Banking Association of North America (HMBANA). HMBANA member banks must follow stringent guidelines based on recommendations from the U.S. Centers for Disease Control and Prevention and updated yearly and take additional precautions to protect against the transmission of infectious diseases (Arnold & Tully, 1996).

The decision to provide formula is best guided by a pediatrician or pediatric health care specialist to ensure the most suitable product for the infant. Research to improve the nutritional content, quality, and digestibility of commercial formulas has evolved over many decades and is ongoing. The Food and Drug Administration bases its regulations of infant formula on standards for infant formulas developed by the American Academy of Pediatrics Committee on Nutrition. Today's formulas are designed to simulate human milk and provide essential proteins, fats, carbohydrates, vitamins, and minerals. Thus, the choice to provide formula instead of human milk during the first months is certainly a viable option. Formula can also be used as a supplement for breast milk when the mother must be away or chooses to omit a feeding or when the mother's breast milk is inadequate. In addition, there are special-purpose formulas for specific nutritional or medical needs.

To ensure optimal benefit from formula feeding, formula must be mixed according to the directions supplied by the manufacturer and prescribed by the infant's pediatrician. Overdiluted formula has less nutritional value and may fill the infant's stomach but not satisfy the infant's hunger; thus, it may fail to provide enough nutrients and calories to sustain growth. Overdilution is often a problem in economically disadvantaged families that dilute the formula to make it last longer and thus reduce its cost. In addition to failing to meet the infant's nutritional needs, overdiluting can lead to water intoxication, a very serious condition that can cause brain swelling and convulsions in infants. Underdiluted formula may also cause problems. Because of water loss through urine, feces, regurgitation, fever, or vomiting, underdiluted formula can fail to meet the infant's need for fluid intake, leading to dehydration and other complications.

Other precautions need to be taken in feeding an infant. Bottle-fed infants must be held in a comfortable position during feeding. The bottle should never be propped. Because the infant lacks the motor skills necessary to move the propped bottle, there is a high risk for choking and asphyxiation. Propping the bottle has other risks as well. When the infant is lying down while bottle feeding, bacteria grow in the pooled liquid in the mouth and cheeks, then make their way to the eustachian tubes, resulting in painful and potentially damaging inner ear infections. Tooth decay in older infants can also occur when formula stays in the mouth too long, coating the teeth with sugars.

Infants' psychological need to be held when being fed is also important. Whether breast- or bottle-fed, infants experience both physical and emotional closeness to their parent or caregiver while being held and cuddled during feeding. Calm, unhurried feeding times contribute to the infant's sense of well-being and trust and enhance the bond between infant and caregiver.

Sensitivity to the infant's hunger and **satiety** cues also enhances infants' trust in both themselves and their caregivers. Overfeeding or underfeeding

**satiety:**
the feeling of having consumed sufficient food to satisfy hunger

results when adults fail to recognize these cues. Turning the head away from a nipple, facial expressions of distaste, and other bodily attempts to refuse food are the infant's way of communicating satiety. Allowing infants to eat what they need without insisting on further intake helps infants to recognize their own feelings of hunger or fullness. Adults must also avoid giving food indiscriminately in an attempt to curtail crying. Not all crying is hunger-related. Providing food or drink every time the child cries establishes a pattern of satisfying discomforts, regardless of what they are, by eating. The obvious outcome of this misguided behavior is obesity and poor physical and psychosocial health.

For most healthy infants, feeding schedules break into four-hour intervals. Some infants may need to be fed every three hours; smaller infants will need food every two hours. Caregivers soon learn to adjust to these rhythms, knowing that as the infant grows and matures, the schedule will become more predictable.

*Solid Foods.*    Taking in solid foods is a different developmental task than sucking and swallowing liquids. Now the infant must mouth or chew the food to soften it, experience its texture as well as its taste, move it to the back of the mouth, and successfully swallow it. This task is not always well coordinated, as is demonstrated by the infant's need for a bib.

Contrary to a somewhat common belief, early introduction of solid foods does not assist the infant in sleeping through the night. Hunger does awaken infants in the night, but nutritionists advise that the decision to introduce solid foods must be based on the infant's need for the nutrients provided by solid foods and on the infant's physiological readiness to handle solid foods, which usually emerges between five and six months of age.

The introduction of solid foods usually begins with iron-fortified cereals. New foods are introduced one at a time, and usually once a week, to accustom the infant to this new experience and to detect any allergic reaction to specific foods. As the intake of solid foods increases, the need for milk or formula decreases. Neither sugar nor salt should be added to foods given to infants; their immature digestive systems do not handle added seasonings well.

As the infant grows and learns to eat a variety of foods, care must be given to providing a balanced diet consisting of foods selected from the vegetable, fruit, meat, grain, and cereal groups. Foods selected for the youngest eaters should be appealing in color, flavor, texture, and shape. Self-feeding foods, foods that can be held in the hand or grasped from a tray, must be easy to chew and swallow. Mealtimes should be unhurried and pleasant.

In providing solid foods to an infant, several precautions must be taken. Foremost is avoiding food contamination. Foods should be fresh and properly stored. Adults must observe scrupulously hygienic procedures for preparing and serving baby meals: washed hands; clean utensils; foods kept at appropriate hot or cold temperatures; and covered, sanitary, and refrigerated storage of unused portions. It is best not to reheat leftover baby food, since illness is caused by microorganisms that grow in foods at room temperature.

**clostridium botulism:**
bacterium that causes botulism

**botulism:**
an often fatal form of food poisoning

Some foods cause particular problems for infants and young children. For instance, honey and corn syrup have been found to contain **clostridium botulinum,** the organism responsible for **botulism.** In infants under a year old, the immature gastrointestinal tract allows this organism to become active and potentially lethal (Christian & Gregor, 1988). Foods that have caused choking include hot dogs and other chunks of meat, peanuts, grapes, raisins, hard or chewy candy, carrots, popcorn, and chewing gum. Selection of nutritional substitutes for these foods and close supervision as the infant learns to handle new foods are imperative. Infants and small children should not be given foods to eat in a moving vehicle or as they are toddling about, as this increases the risk of choking.

Contemporary concerns about obesity, cholesterol, and other diet-related health problems have led some parents to mistakenly believe that reducing fat and calories in the infant's diet is necessary. Quite the contrary is true. Body size, proportions, and composition are in a period of very rapid change. The infant's calorie needs per unit of body weight far exceed those of older children and adults to maintain rapid growth. In the absence of teeth, infants depend on consuming sufficient amounts of breast milk or formula to meet their increased caloric needs. In addition, during the last trimester of prenatal development and during the first few years of postnatal development, myelination of nerve fibers takes place. Fat is a major component of myelin (the tissue that surrounds the nerves as they mature) and, as such, is an essential part of the infant's diet if optimal neurological integrity is to be obtained. The American Academy of Pediatrics (1993) advises against practices that limit the diets of infants.

*Colic.*    *Colic* is abdominal discomfort that occurs in infants two weeks to three months of age. It is characterized by irritability, fussing, or crying sometimes for more than three hours a day and occurring as often as three days a week. It can be quite painful for the infant and distressing to parents. Why colic begins to appear at this age is unclear. Some suggested causes are swallowed air, high-carbohydrate foods, overfeeding, intolerance for cow's milk, intestinal allergy, a stressful environment, or impending illness (Pilliteri, 1992). Some infants seem more prone to colic than others, and no universal treatment exists, since the causes vary. Physical examination by a pediatrician may be needed to determine whether more serious problems exist.

Some preventive measures can be taken to reduce the incidence of colic. These include feeding in an unhurried and calm manner, burping at regular intervals during feeding, avoiding either overfeeding or underfeeding, and, with a physician's help, identifying possible food allergies. When colic occurs, holding the infant upright or lying the infant prone across the lap may be helpful. Sometimes, changing caregivers helps. A tired and frustrated parent or caregiver whose attempts to soothe the infant have met with failure may, if these efforts continue, exacerbate the problem.

## Safety

The infant's growing mobility and inclination to put things in the mouth presupposes a number of health and safety issues. The most common safety concerns during the first year are automobile accidents, falls, burns, choking or suffocation, poisonings, and drowning. Adult failure to recognize the infant's changing abilities and curiosities is often the reason infants get injured. The infant's surroundings must be sanitary and frequently examined for potential dangers: objects on the floor that could scratch, cut, or go into the mouth (e.g., balloons, coins, marbles, small toy parts, buttons, safety pins); exposed electrical outlets and electrical wires that could be pulled or mouthed; furnishings

*Proper use of approved infant safety seats helps to prevent serious injuries or death.*

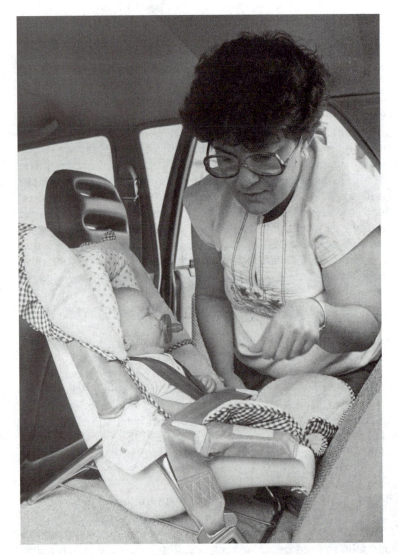

that topple easily; toxic substances within easy reach (e.g., medicines, cosmetics, household cleaning and gardening supplies, arts and crafts products); poisonous plants; swimming pools, bathtubs, and other bodies of water; hot water faucets and unsanitary toilet bowls; and many others.

All baby equipment and clothing should be selected according to current safety standards. These standards apply to bassinets, cribs, car seats, carriages, swings, playpens, walkers, jogging strollers, pacifiers, toys, and all other baby supplies and equipment. The Consumer Products Safety Commission regularly publishes information about safe products for children and items that have been recalled because of the hazards they pose. Parents and caregivers can avail themselves of this information at no cost, a responsible thing to do to prevent unnecessary (and sometimes lethal) injuries to infants and children. (See the Further Readings and Resources at the end of this chapter.)

Beginning in infancy, automobile child safety seats must be consistently used in transporting an infant or young child in a motor vehicle. Responding to the fact that more children are killed and injured in automobile accidents than from any other type of injury, every state now requires that infants and children be properly restrained when riding in a vehicle. Proper use of infant safety seats helps to prevent death and injury. The Federal Motor Vehicle Safety Standard Act 213 mandates that passenger safety seats manufactured after January 1981 must meet certain standards for design and use. However, this law did not prohibit the sale of infant passenger seats manufactured before this date. Consequently, some unsafe infant passenger seats may still be on the market through hand-me-downs, garage sales, and thrift shops. Since September 1, 1995, the National Highway Traffic Safety Administration has required that all manual safety belts have a lockable feature to lock them securely around child safety seats and that they be properly tethered to the adult seat back. Many automobile manufacturers now have integrated safety seats for children and other automobile child safety features.

The safest place for children of all ages to ride is in the back seat of a vehicle. Infants should never be placed in the front seat of a vehicle that has a passenger air bag. Infants should ride facing the back of the car until they are one year old and weigh at least 20 pounds. Belt-positioning booster seats with lap/shoulder belt securing can be used for older and larger babies. Car seat manufacturer's instructions should be conscientiously followed, since incorrectly installed and secured car seats place children at risk in the event of a sudden stop or accident. Begin consistent (never wavering) use of car seats and restraints in infancy, and as children get older, the use of appropriate vehicle safety restraints will become an established habit.

Wise selection of toys for infants involves choosing toys that are constructed of pieces too large to swallow, are lightweight and easily grasped, and are free of sharp edges, projectiles, batteries, or small removable parts. They should be made of washable, nontoxic materials and should be sturdy enough to withstand vigorous play. Toys should be selected for their sensory appeal and should be age appropriate for the infant who will play with them.

## Opportunities to Interact, Explore, and Play

Each new motor skill extends the infant's ability to interact with people and objects in the environment. Infants enjoy looking at colorful objects in the environment. They enjoy listening to the human voice and to recordings of pleasing or familiar sounds and music and experiencing different textures such as soft toys, bedding, carpeting, and so on. Toys and focused interactions in which infant and parent or caregiver talk, laugh, imitate each other, play peek-a-boo and pat-a-cake, explore the surroundings, label objects and events, and share pictures and cloth or board books all provide opportunities to play, learn, and develop social competence. Play is essential to all facets of growth and development: physical/motor, psychosocial, cognitive, language, and literacy. We will discuss play and play behaviors in the context of these developmental areas throughout the text.

## Socioeconomic Influences

Adequate food, clothing, and shelter depend on socioeconomic circumstances. Availability of and access to medical and preventive health care, good nutrition, child care, educational opportunities, and other community resources are essential to healthy growth and development. Though the overall poverty rate for children under six dropped from 26 percent in 1993 to 22 percent in 1997, unfortunately, many U.S. families continue to live in poverty today. Infants and children in these families are far more at risk for poor growth and developmental outcomes than other children (Children's Defense Fund, 1999; National Center for Children in Poverty, 1999.)

## HEALTH AND WELL-BEING ISSUES IN INFANT DEVELOPMENT

### Infant Mortality Rates and Risks

**syndrome:**
a group of combined symptoms that characterize a physiological or psychological disorder

Infant mortality rates (deaths during the first year of life) in the United States appear to be decreasing but remain alarmingly high for a modern industrialized and technologically advanced nation. Despite great strides in medical and child health protection over the years, in 1998 the infant mortality rate for all races was 7.2 deaths per 1,000 live births. However, this rate is down from the 1991 infant mortality rate of 8.9 per 1,000 live births (Federal Interagency Forum on Child and Family Statistics, 1999). In the United States, an African-American infant is more than twice as likely to die during the first year as an Anglo infant (Children's Defense Fund, 1999). The causes of neonatal and infant deaths among all races relate to poor prenatal and newborn care, prematurity and low birth weight, congenital malformations and diseases, complications associated with certain **syndromes,** including fetal alcohol syndrome, fetal tobacco syndrome, fetal marijuana syndrome, chemical withdrawal syndrome, and sudden infant death syndrome. The damaging effects of alcohol, tobacco, and drugs have been discussed in previous chapters. However, a brief discussion of SIDS at this point might be helpful.

Sudden infant death syndrome (SIDS) is the sudden and unexpected death of an apparently healthy infant during the first year. SIDS accounts for 6,000–7,000 infant deaths each year in the United States (American Academy of Pediatrics Committee on Child Abuse and Neglect, 1994). It is the most common cause of death between the ages of one and twelve months and most common age of occurrence is between two and four months.

In the past, it was thought that infants who died in their cribs had smothered in their covers (thus the term *crib death*). However, since its identification as a syndrome in the 1960s, this perplexing phenomenon has commanded considerable research, and its actual cause or causes are still difficult to pinpoint.

**apnea:**
absence of breathing for a period of up to 20 seconds

In their rigorous yet elusive search for causes over the past three decades, scientists have identified a number of factors associated with SIDS. While these factors are not causes in themselves, they have helped researchers to identify high-risk populations. The following factors have been associated with SIDS: prematurity, low birth weight, low APGAR scores, maternal age younger than 20 at first pregnancy or younger than 25 during subsequent pregnancies, an interval of less than 12 months since the preceding pregnancy, **apnea,** multiple births, cold weather, young mothers who have had poor prenatal care, low socioeconomic status, a maternal history of smoking, drug abuse (particularly methadone), anemia, and siblings who died of SIDS; in a small proportion of SIDS cases, child abuse is suspected (American Academy of Pediatrics Committee on Child Abuse and Neglect, 1994).

A number of theories have attempted to explain SIDS. Some have implicated heredity; others have suggested upper respiratory viruses or a bacterium such as botulism; still others have proposed **metabolic** disorders, allergies, **hyperthermia** and **hypothermia**, and central nervous system abnormalities. One popular explanation relates to the infant's cardiovascular system. Studies have found, in a number of cases, an abnormality in the way the brain regulates breathing and heart rate (C. E. Hunt & Brouillette, 1987). However, not all infants studied exhibited this abnormality, so this theory awaits additional research. In spite of years of research, scientists are still unable to identify a specific cause or causes.

The incidence of SIDS appears to have decreased in recent years, owing in part to a "Back to Sleep" campaign launched in 1994 by the National Institute of Child Health and Human Development and the American Academy of Pediatrics. The Back to Sleep campaign has attempted to educate parents and child care personnel about SIDS and the importance of placing infants on their sides (with a rolled blanket for a prop, if necessary) or on their backs to sleep, as a preventive strategy, rather than on their stomachs. This practice is now widespread, and the reduction in the incidence of SIDS has been attributed to it.

**metabolic:** pertains to the body's complex chemical conversion of food into substances and energy necessary for maintenance of life

**hyperthermia:** a very high body temperature

**hypothermia:** a below-normal body temperature

## Abuse and Neglect

Legally, abuse and neglect are defined in the United States as "the physical or mental injury, sexual abuse, negligent treatment, or maltreatment of a child under the age of eighteen by a person who is responsible for the child's welfare under circumstances which indicate that the child's health or welfare is harmed or threatened thereby" (Child Abuse Prevention and Treatment Act of 1975, 42 U.S. Code 5101).

Abuse takes many forms: physical, in which bodily injury is inflicted; psychological, in which a child is cursed, berated, ignored, or rejected; and sexual abuse, which ranges from exposure and fondling to incest and rape. The victims of sexual abuse are sometimes infants. Studies have found that infants and children under age three are particularly susceptible to child abuse (Mayhall & Norgard, 1983). Frustrations over infant crying, colic, diaper soiling, eating, sleeping, and other stresses, as well as maternal depression, family stress, and lack of knowledge about child development, may provoke an abusive adult. A common form of infant abuse is known as shaken baby syndrome and appears mostly in infants younger than six months of age. Shaking an infant or small child can cause serious physical and mental damage and even death.

**Failure to thrive** in infancy due to maternal deprivation or neglect has been documented. Studies have shown that some children who are raised in impoverished or neglectful conditions during the first year of life show signs of severe developmental retardation (Province & Lipton, 1962) and impaired neurological development (Perry, 1998). These infants exhibit delayed physical growth and skeletal development, resulting in heights and weights far below those expected for their ages (Barbero & Shaheen, 1967). Neglected children are more susceptible to disease, have more gastrointestinal upsets, and are particularly emotionally vulnerable.

**failure to thrive:** a condition in which an apparently healthy infant fails to grow normally

Neglect may take different forms, such as inadequate dietary practices, which impede growth, and failure to provide other necessities such as clothing, shelter, supervision, and protection. Sometimes neglect includes denial of medical attention. Intellectual stimulation and emotional support may also be absent. Some infants are simply abandoned.

Abuse and neglect occur at all socioeconomic levels, in all ethnic groups, and in all types of families: one-parent, two-parent, extended, large, and small. The incidence of abuse and neglect in families can be cyclical. Children who have been abused may become abusive adults (Gelles & Edfeldt, 1990), though intervention such as counseling and therapy, education, support groups for families, and subsequent positive life experiences may break the cycle. In some cases, children need to be removed from situations of neglect or abuse. Today, all states have child abuse reporting laws under which suspected child abuse must be reported to appropriate authorities.

## Infants with Special Needs

Throughout infancy and early childhood, there may be warning signs that an infant or young child is not growing and developing according to expected progressions and timetables. Infants whose prenatal development was less than optimal owing to the challenges of poverty, maternal health complications, inadequate nutrition, or teratogenic disturbances to fetal development or those who suffered prematurity or other birth trauma are most often infants identified as being at risk. That is, their growth and development is expected to be marked with challenges that may require specialized care, treatment, and educational practices. Infants who are at risk for poor or delayed development or who have disabling conditions require assessment and identification that can lead to diagnosis and intervention as early as possible. The Apgar Scale, the Brazelton Neonatal Behavioral Assessment Scale, the Bayley Scales of Infant Development, and the Bayley Infant Neurodevelopmental Screener are examples of tests that are frequently used to provide initial and diagnostic information.

In addition to earliest possible intervention, infants with special needs require knowledge and special sensitivity on the part of their caregivers. Sometimes, the challenges of caring for an infant with special needs can be daunting for parents, family members, and nonparental caregivers. Today, Part C (formerly Part H): Early Intervention Program for Infants and Toddlers with Disabilities (Birth through age two) of the Individuals with Disabilities Education Act (IDEA) provides federal funds to states for services specifically for birth through age two and provides funds to develop, establish and maintain a statewide system that offers early intervention services. The law provides for the following groups of children:

1. Infants and children who have a measurable developmental delay in one or more of the following developmental domains; cognitive, physical, language/communication, social, emotional, and adaptive, or self-help behavior

2. Children who have a diagnosed physical or mental condition that could result in a developmental delay (e.g., Down syndrome, multiple sclerosis, sensory impairments, cerebral palsy, autism)

3. Children who are at risk of experiencing developmental delay, as determined by the state, if intervention is not provided

Recognizing the importance of the family in the child's development, the law provides for services to help families through counseling and other services and mandates that intervention services be provided in the types of settings in which infants and toddlers without disabilities would participate. This means that child care programs, nursery schools, public schools, and family care settings must make provisions to successfully integrate infants and toddlers with special needs into their programs. This includes providing additional and sometimes specialized training for adults who are responsible for the children, developing appropriate communicative and interactive skills, adapting physical environments, integrating remediation and intervention strategies into a developmentally appropriate curriculum, and working effectively with parents.

## Nonparental Infant Care

Nonparental child care is a necessity for millions of U.S. families. It is estimated that each day, 13 million children spend a part or all of their day in nonparental care, and many of these children have been enrolled by 11 weeks of age (G. C. Adams & Poersch, 1997). Because the first three years of life are critical ones and because parents are increasingly depending on child care, it is essential that nonparental care be of the highest quality. High-quality child care is expensive and is more expensive for infants and toddlers than for older children. Wise selection of child care for infants and toddlers involves seeking well-trained, knowledgeable, and sensitive adults who have the personal qualities a parent determines will be good for their child. Adult-to-child ratios in group programs serving infants and toddlers ideally should be no more than one adult to three children. The home or center should meet health and safety standards, and the daily routines should be warm, supportive, infant-friendly, stimulating, and satisfying. Good-quality nonparental child care can be an enormous source of comfort to parents who need it. However, many families lack knowledge about how to choose good-quality child care, and the cost of such care often exceeds the family's ability to pay for it.

Those who provide infant care have a moral and ethical responsibility to be knowledgeable about infants' needs and the critical nature of early neurological and physiological development and the essential experiences needed to foster optimal growth and development. Through state licensing laws and standards, accreditation standards of the National Association for the Education of Young Children, and standards such as those set by the joint efforts of the American Public Health Association and the American Academy of Pediatrics (1992), providers can assess their facilities, programs, and interactive environments and make continuous efforts to improve and enrich their programs so that parents who enlist their services can be confident in the choices they have made.

*Role of the Early Childhood Professional*

*Facilitating Physical and Motor Development in Infants*

1. Provide adequate and appropriate food, clothing, and shelter.
2. Access professional medical and health care supervision.
3. Be ever vigilant for infants who may need early identification and assessment of special needs and timely intervention.
4. Provide sanitary and safe surroundings for the growing and curious infant.
5. Provide sensorimotor stimulation through engaging interactions, sensory-rich environments, and opportunities to explore.
6. Provide an encouraging, supportive, and predictable atmosphere of love, acceptance, and socially and emotionally satisfying interactions.
7. Provide guidance that is positive and instructive in helping the increasingly mobile infant to discover his or her capabilities in an atmosphere of both physical and psychological protection and safety.
8. Establish collaborative and supportive relationships with parents of infants.
9. Stay abreast of health and safety alerts, regulations, and laws to protect infants and young children.
10. Become aware of community resources that address the needs of infants and their families.

# KEY TERMS

apnea
atrophy
axon
behaviorist
botulism
cephalocaudal
cerebral cortex
clostridium botulinum
colostrum
dendrite
developmental
  interactionist
  perspective
embryonic cell mass
failure to thrive

fontanelles
glial
hyperthermia
hypothermia
kinesthesis
maturationist
metabolic
myelin
neonatal period
neural tube
neuron
neurotransmitter
ossify
perception
plasticity

primitive reflex
proximodistal
psychological state
reflex
satiety
skeletal age
subcortical
survival reflex
synapse
syndrome
systems approach
temperament
transactionalist perspective
vernix caseosa

# REVIEW STRATEGIES AND ACTIVITIES

1. Review the key terms individually or with a classmate.
2. Compare infant formulas and baby foods that are available at your local supermarket. What nutrients are listed on the labels and in what proportions? How do these foods differ? How are they alike? What considerations are essential in the selection of a formula or solid food for individual infants?

3. Invite a child protective services professional from your state or regional health and human resources department to talk to the class about child abuse and neglect. What is the responsibility of the early childhood professional in dealing with abuse and neglect of young children?

4. Visit an accredited child care center or a family day care home that cares primarily for infants. Make a list of health and safety precautions practiced by the child caregivers and staff in these settings.

5. Identify and investigate support services and infant care programs for infants with special needs and their families.

6. Discuss with your classmates the issues surrounding infant health and safety and identify ways the early childhood professional can address these issues.

# FURTHER READINGS

American Public Health Association and American Academy of Pediatrics. (1992). *Caring for our children: National health and safety performance standards: Guidelines for out-of-home child care programs.* Washington, DC, and Elk Grove Village, IL: Authors.

Barry, V. M., & Cantor, P. (Eds.) (1998). *ACEI Newsletter: Focus on Infants & Toddlers, 11* (2). (Theme issue on infants and toddlers "at risk")

Columbia University School of Public Health, National Center for Children in Poverty. (1997). *Poverty and brain development in early childhood. Fact Sheet.* New York: Author.

Dietz, W. H., & Stern, L. (Eds.). (1999). *Guide to your child's nutrition.* Elk Grove Village, IL: American Academy of Pediatrics.

Klass, C. S. (1999). *The child care provider: Promoting young children's development.* Baltimore, MD: Paul H. Brookes.

Pennsylvania Chapter of the American Academy of Pediatrics. (1997). *Model child care health policies* (Rev. ed.). Washington, DC: National Association for the Education of Young Children.

Schiff, D., & Shelov, S. P. (1997). *Guide to your child's symptoms: Birth through adolescence.* Elk Grove Village, IL: American Academy of Pediatrics.

Shevlov, S. P. (1998). *Your baby's first year.* Elk Grove IL: American Academy of Pediatrics.

# OTHER RESOURCES

*Focus on Infants and Toddlers, 0 to 3,* Newsletter
Association for Childhood Education International
17904 Georgia Ave., Ste. 215
Oiney, MD 20832.
*Pediatrics for Parents Newsletter.* P. O. Box 1069, Bangor, ME 04402-1069.
The Consumer Product Safety Commission
4340 East West Highway, Suite 502, Bethesda, MD 20814-4408
Http://www.cpsc.gov/
Hotline: 1-800-638-2772
Alliance to End Childhood Lead Poisoning
*http://www.aec/p.org*
Child Care Aware
http://www.naccrra.net/childcareaware/index.htm

# CHAPTER SIX

## Psychosocial Development of the Infant

*The first cry of a newborn baby in Chicago or Zamboango, in Amsterdam or Rangoon, has the same pitch and key, each saying, I am! I have come through! I belong! I am a member of the Family!*

CARL SANDBURG

*Recent brain research suggests that warm, responsive care is not only comforting for an infant; it is critical to healthy development.*

RIMA SHORE

*After studying this chapter, you will demonstrate comprehension by:*

▶ Identifying important theories associated with psychosocial development.

▶ Describing the potential effects of earliest psychosocial experiences on brain growth and early neurological development.

▶ Relating the concept of essential experiences to psychosocial development during the first year.

▶ Identifying major social and emotional milestones in infancy.

▶ Describing factors that influence psychosocial development.

▶ Describing the role of adults in facilitating healthy psychosocial development in the infant.

Listen to the musings of parents as they attempt to define personality characteristics in their newborns:

"He has such a peaceful look on his face."

"She is very squirmy."

"When he cries, he really wants to be heard!"

"She is such an easy baby."

"He is much more alert than his sister was."

What do these early observations tell us about an infant's personality, emotions, or future social behaviors? What are the influences of heredity and environment on psychosocial development? Can early emotional and social experiences influence the organizational and functional capacities of the developing brain, and hence the type of person the child can become? What meaning do infants make of their experiences and interactions with others? What constitutes sound mental health in infancy? What role do adults, siblings, and playmates play in enhancing a child's opportunities to achieve a healthy personality and prosocial attributes? These questions and many more spark our interest in the psychosocial development of human beings. This chapter is concerned with the types of behaviors and experiences in infancy that promote or thwart healthy psychosocial development.

## THEORIES OF PSYCHOSOCIAL DEVELOPMENT

The study of psychology in general and of psychosocial development in particular is concerned with how the human being behaves and what underlying and unseen mental processes shape and direct individual behaviors. In the past, and to a great extent today, research in psychology has relied on careful observation of infants and children in naturalistic settings (home and family contexts, laboratory nursery schools, play therapy settings, and other child care contexts). Studies of the social and emotional actions, reactions, and interactions of infants and young children as they grow, develop, and learn in these varying contexts have yielded invaluable insights. Parenting and child care practices rely heavily on these insights and continuing research of this nature. Complementing naturalistic studies and focusing them toward biological origins has been the research of contemporary neurobiologists. Today, through sophisticated technologies, the biology of psychology has begun to further enlighten scholars and early childhood practitioners about the neurological origins of specific behavioral traits and responses. Contemporary studies of early brain growth and neurological development have the potential for providing precise data on how and when certain behaviors emerge and what types of early experiences enhance or thwart healthy neurological development and subsequently healthy psychosocial behaviors.

The study of psychosocial development then necessarily examines the theoretical perspectives on behavior along with the biology of behavior. Let us begin this discussion by reviewing a few of the major theories that continue to guide thought and practice in early care and education and juxtapose them against emerging brain development research.

## Freud's Psychoanalytic Psychology

**fixation:**
in psychoanalytic theory, a point in development that becomes fixed, failing to move forward to more mature forms

Sigmund Freud (1933) was the first to propose a theory of personality based on underlying psychological structures and needs. Freud believed that behaviors were governed by unconscious desires and hidden motives. He was among the first to propose that personality development proceeded through a series of stages wherein certain conflicts must be successfully resolved before moving on to the next stage. Successful resolution of stage-related conflicts over time should lead to healthy development. Freud advanced the concept of **fixation**, which suggests that individual psychological behaviors can cease to move beyond a particular point in development, carrying immature forms of behaving forward into later stages and resulting in less than healthy psychological growth. Freud believed that early experiences determined the course and nature of later development and behavior. Further, he proposed that individuals are born with psychosexual instincts that change over the years from infancy to maturity. The focus of psychosexual energy relating to these instincts shifts from one part of the body to another as the individual matures. Development is characterized as a series of five stages revealing the shift in psychosexual energy. Table 6.1 describes this sequence. Many psychologists who studied Freud's works argue that he placed too much emphasis on the notion that sexual drives influence personality development. Nevertheless, Freud's scholarship and influence continue to undergird child development theory and practice.

## Erikson's Theory of Psychosocial Development

The psychoanalytic perspective advanced by Freud provides a template for understanding Erik Erikson's theory of personality development. Like Freud, Erikson believed that development progressed through a series of identifiable stages;

---

**TABLE 6.1.   Freud's Psychosexual Stages of Development**

| | |
|---|---|
| Oral stage (1st year) | The primary focus of stimulation is the mouth and oral cavity, and the primary source of gratification is eating, sucking, and biting. The mother (or primary caregiver) is the source of satisfaction of the basic needs of this period. |
| Anal stage (2nd to 4th year) | Elimination and retention of fecal material become the focus of the child's attentions and energies. The child must learn appropriate time and place for elimination. This is the time when the child first learns to conform to social expectations. |
| Phallic stage (4th to 6th year) | Psychic energy is focused on the genital organs and pleasure received through organ manipulation. The realization that one is biologically and psychologically separate from others occurs, and the resolution of conflicts relating to appropriate sex roles becomes an issue. Children are said to develop incestuous desires for the parent of the other sex during this stage. |
| Latency stage (middle childhood) | Energy formerly directed toward sexual concerns becomes channeled in other directions, mainly that of forming affectional and social relationships with parents and other children (usually same-sex friends). |
| Genital stage (adolescence) | Physical sexual changes and development become the center of attention. Sex-role identity becomes a major issue. |

*Source:* Freud (1933).

and like Freud, he explored crucial interactions between children and their caregivers. He too, emphasized the importance of early experiences to later personality development. But Erikson was interested in the larger societal and cultural context in which psychosocial development occurs. By expanding on Freudian theory, Erikson identified eight stages of psychosocial development, each representing stage-related conflicts to be resolved in order to proceed successfully to the next and subsequent stages leading to healthy personality development. His eight stages represent a life span perspective that includes not only developmental changes in infants and children but in adults as well.

The eight stages of personality development Erikson proposed are characterized by basic life conflicts to be resolved. These conflicts result from an individual's biological maturation and expectations imposed on the individual by society. Erikson suggests that critical periods, or developmental crises, are associated with each stage of healthy personality development.

According to Erikson's theory, the first year of life is a critical period for the development of a sense of trust. The conflict for the infant involves striking a balance between trust and mistrust. This primary psychosocial task of infancy provides a developmental foundation from which later stages of personality development can emerge. It is represented in Figure 6.1 as the first stage in Erikson's eight-stage theory. Resolution of the trust/mistrust conflict is manifest in a mature personality in behaviors that basically trust (themselves and others) but maintain a healthy amount of skepticism.

Infants learn to trust when their caregiving is characterized by nurturance, warmth, and predictability. Needs for food, comfort, and satisfying interactions

**FIGURE 6.1**
Erikson's Eight
Psychosocial
Stages

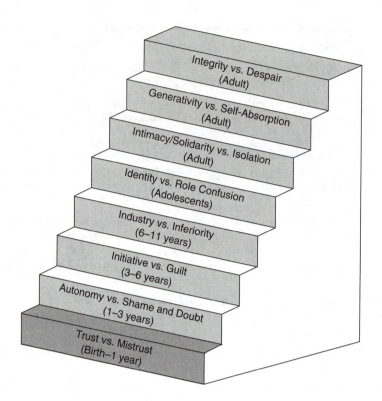

with others depend on a responsive and protective environment. The infant's first experiences of being fed when hungry, held and stroked soothingly when fretful, changed when diapers are soiled, protected from insult or injury, and played with when bored establish the basis for a developing sense of trust. Infants must be able to depend on their caregivers to come when beckoned; to interact with them in warm, supportive and affectionate ways; and to respond appropriately to their various physiological, social, and emotional needs. When caregiving is responsive to infant cues, infants learn to trust their own ability to signal needs and to elicit responses from caregivers. This helps to establish not only a trust in others, but also a trust in oneself. The infant who has established a healthy sense of trust is better equipped for the next stage, developing a sense of autonomy. Autonomy builds upon a basic sense of trust and emerges during the toddler period of development described in Chapter 9.

Mistrust arises when the infant's caregivers fail to adequately respond to cues of hunger, discomfort, boredom, and other needs or do so in inconsistent and unpredictable ways. Infants who are subjected to neglect, rejection, or inappropriate expectations or infants who are repeatedly left to "cry it out" learn that other people cannot be trusted. Equally detrimental is the failure to learn to trust oneself and to gain a sense of self from positive and responsive interactions with others achieved by one's own efforts. Failure to develop a sturdy sense of trust undermines the ability to succeed in resolving the autonomy versus shame and doubt psychosocial challenge during the toddler period.

Facilitating the developing sense of trust is the infant's increasing cognitive abilities. During this first year, the infant comes to realize that persons and objects exist even though they may not be present. Piaget (1952) considered this a major milestone in cognitive development and termed it *object permanence.* The infant's appreciation of object permanence helps him or her to realize that parents or caregivers exist even when they cannot be seen and that they can be trusted to return when summoned. The development of a sense of object permanence is discussed in greater detail in Chapter 7 as it relates to cognitive development.

## Attachment Theory

The subject of infant bonding and **attachment** has received considerable attention in both the professional and the popular press in recent years. Recall from Chapter 4 that *bonding* refers to the strong emotional tie between the mother or father (or caregiver) and the infant, usually thought to occur in the early days or weeks after delivery. Attachment emerges gradually during the first year and may be an outgrowth of the parent-infant bond. It is based on the quality of the interactions between the child and the parent or primary caregiver.

During the 1950s and early 1960s, John Bowlby, a psychiatrist and pioneer in the study of attachment, published a series of papers based on extensive research on mother-child attachments and separations. These papers, later enlarged and refined, were published in three volumes (Bowlby, 1969/1982, 1973, 1980) and have provided the impetus for much scholarly research and discussion.

Studying children who had been raised in institutions, Bowlby focused on their inability to form lasting relationships with others. Bowlby attributed this inability to the lack of opportunity to form an attachment to a mother or mother figure during infancy. He also studied children who, after experiencing strong

**attachment:**
a strong emotional relationship between two people, characterized by mutual affection and a desire to maintain proximity

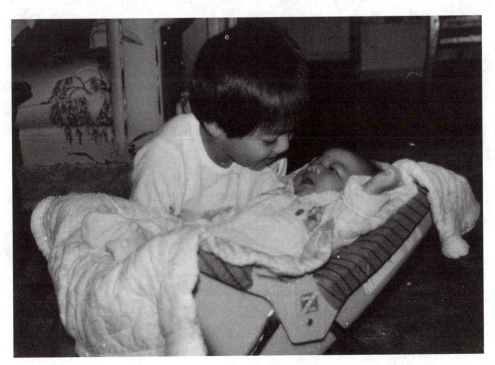

*Social responses become more reciprocal as infants get older.*

infant-mother attachments, were separated from their mothers for extended periods of time. He observed that these children also developed resistance to close human ties. Bowlby was convinced that to understand these behaviors, one should examine infant-mother attachments.

In the institutions in which the subjects of Bowlby's studies lived, staff members tended adequately to their custodial responsibilities of feeding, clothing, bathing, and overseeing the infants' safety. They did not necessarily respond to the infants in affectionate and nurturing ways. Staff members did not respond to infants' cries or return their smiles, nor did they coo and babble with them or carry them about. Even though their physical needs were being met, infants in these settings failed or were severely impaired in their ability to relate to caregivers. Studies of attachment highlight the critical need to form these attachments during the early months and years and suggest that failure to do so may have a lifelong effect on healthy social and emotional development (Ainsworth, 1973; Bowlby, 1973; Bretherton & Walters, 1985).

Bowlby (1969/1982, pp. 265–330) proposed a sequence for the development of attachment between the infant and others. The sequence is divided into four phases:

### Phase 1 (Birth to 8–12 Weeks): Indiscriminate Responsiveness to Humans.
During this phase, infants orient to people in their environment, visually tracking them, grasping and reaching for them, and smiling and babbling. The infant often stops crying on seeing a face or hearing a voice. These behaviors sustain the attentions of others and thus their proximity to the infant, which is the infant's goal.

### Phase 2 (3–6 Months): Focusing on Familiar People.
The infant's behaviors toward others remain virtually the same except that they are more marked in relation to the mother or perhaps the father. Social responses begin to become more selective, however, the social smile being reserved for familiar people, while strangers receive a long, intent stare. Cooing, babbling, and gurgling are more readily elicited by familiar people. A principal attachment figure begins to emerge; this is usually the mother.

### Phase 3 (6 Months to 3 Years): Active Proximity Seeking.
Infants show greater discrimination in their interactions with people. They become deeply concerned for the attachment person's presence and cry when that person starts to leave. Infants will monitor the attachment person's movements, calling out to the person or using whatever means of locomotion they have to maintain proximity to the person. The attachment person serves as a base from which to explore and is followed when departing and greeted warmly upon return. Certain other people may become subsidiary attachment figures; however, strangers are now treated with caution and will soon evoke emotions of alarm and withdrawal.

**separation anxiety:** fear of being separated from the attachment person

During phase 3, two very predictable fears emerge. **Separation anxiety** occurs as the relationship between the infant and the attachment person becomes more intense and exclusive. The infant cries, sometimes quite vociferously, on the departure of the attachment person and exhibits intense joy on reunion. Although this phase can be disconcerting for parents and primary caregivers, it is

**FIGURE 6.2**
A Sensitive Response to Separation Anxiety

- Recognize that new experiences present new challenges for the infant; some of these challenges can be quite unsettling, maybe even alarming.
- Provide predictable, unhurried schedules, particularly when introducing the infant to new experiences.
- Begin to accustom the infant to short separations at home by
  - Maintaining visual and auditory contact by leaving the infant's door open at nap and bedtimes
  - Maintaining voice contact across rooms and, when departing the room of a protesting infant, providing softly spoken verbal assurances
- Ritualize bedtimes and naptimes; e.g., provide a slower pace, softened volume on TV, bath and change of clothing, brush teeth, read a story, rock and sing, kiss goodnight, and tuck in bed.
- Provide prior opportunities for the infant to become familiar with a new babysitter or child care arrangement.
- Select caregivers on the basis of their ability to respond to the infant's unique rhythms and temperament.
- Familiarize the caregiver with the infant's routines and preferences.
- Have available for the infant any special blanket, stuffed toy, or other object from which the infant gains comfort.
- Ritualize departure time: hug, kiss, spoken good-byes, wave, and so on. Never slip away when the child is not looking; rather, let the infant develop confidence in the arrangement.
- Anticipate the new experience with pleasure.
- Be dependable. First separations should be brief, and reunions should be unwaveringly predictable.

**FIGURE 6.2**
A Sensitive Response to Separation Anxiety

nevertheless, a healthy aspect of psychosocial development. To the extent that adults respond to separation anxiety in supportive and empathic ways, the child can gain trust and confidence in their caregivers and in their own self-comforting strategies. Figure 6.2 offers suggestions for caregivers during this difficult phase.

**Stranger anxiety** is another characteristic fear of phase 3. Occurring around seven to eight months of age, the infant's stranger anxiety is characterized by lengthy stares and subsequent crying at the sight of an unfamiliar person. Alarmed, the infant will cling tightly to the attachment person and resist letting go. Stranger anxiety, like separation anxiety, signals maturing cognitive and psychosocial development and can lead to healthy trust and mistrust when responded to in supportive and helpful ways. Figure 6.3 includes suggestions for dealing with stranger anxiety.

**stranger anxiety:** fear of strangers characterized by avoidance, crying, or other distress signals

### Phase 4 (3 Years to the End of Childhood): Partnership Behavior.
Before this phase, the child is unable to consider the attachment person's intentions. For instance, the suggestion that "I will be right back" is meaningless to the child, who will insist on going along anyway. By age three, the child has developed a greater understanding of parental intent and can envision the parent's behavior while separated. The child is now more willing and able to let go and can be more flexible.

**FIGURE 6.3**
A Sensitive Response to Stranger Anxiety

Learning to distinguish mother and father from others is an important task in infancy, and for many of today's infants, adapting to a nonparental caregiver may be an added task. The parent or caregiver must recognize that fears in the first year relate to new learnings and limited experiences.

- Discourage the unfamiliar person from attempting to hold the baby.
- Provide ample time for the infant to assess the stranger and sense your reaction to him or her.
- When introducing the infant to a new caregiver, invite the person to visit. Spend time together, allowing the infant time to accept this new person into his or her world.
- During this session, let yourself serve as the secure base from which the infant can venture forth to make friendly overtures with the new acquaintance.
- Allow the infant to "control" the encounter, deciding when to approach and when to retreat.
- Provide the infant with familiar and comforting objects to hold.
- The confidence of older siblings who are already familiar with the "stranger" may encourage the infant's comfort and acceptance.

Mary Ainsworth has studied differences in attachment behaviors (1967, 1973; Ainsworth, Blehar, Waters, & Wall, 1978; Ainsworth & Wittig, 1969). Using her Strange Situation test, Ainsworth and her colleagues attempted to delineate individual differences in the quality of attachments that infants form. She devised a series of eight episodes (Table 6.2) designed to induce increasing anxiety in the infant. She recorded and analyzed exploratory behaviors, reactions to strangers, reactions to separation, and infant behaviors on reuniting with the mother after separation.

From her studies, Ainsworth identified three categories of attachment:

1. Insecure attachment: anxious and avoidant
2. Secure attachment
3. Insecure attachment: anxious and resistant

Securely attached infants were found to be visibly upset upon separation from the mother and greeted her heartily and sought close physical contact with her on reunion. In their mother's presence, these infants more willingly explored their environments and were friendly with the stranger.

Insecurely attached, anxious/avoidant infants showed little distress when the mother departed and no great joy upon her return, generally avoiding contact with her. With strangers, they behaved similarly, tending to avoid or ignore them.

Insecurely attached, anxious/resistant infants were less likely to explore when the mother was present and were distressed when she departed. The reunion was strained as the infant maintained proximity but resisted the mother's efforts at physical contact, displaying apparent anger at her absence. These infants were quite wary of strangers, even with the mother present.

**TABLE 6.2. Eight Episodes That Make Up the Strange Situations Test**

| Episode Number | Persons Present | Duration | Brief Description of Action |
|---|---|---|---|
| 1 | Mother, baby, and observer | 30 seconds | Observer introduces mother and baby to experimental room, then leaves. (Room contains many appealing toys scattered about.) |
| 2 | Mother and baby | 3 minutes | Mother is nonparticipant while baby explores; if necessary, play is stimulated after 2 minutes. |
| 3 | Stranger, mother, and baby | 3 minutes | Stranger enters. First minute; stranger silent. Second minute; stranger converses with mother. Third minute; stranger approaches baby. After 3 minutes mother leaves unobtrusively. |
| 4 | Stranger and baby | 3 minutes or less | First separation episode. Stranger's behavior is geared to that of baby. |
| 5 | Mother and baby | 3 minutes or more | First reunion episode. Mother greets and/or comforts the baby, then tries to settle him again in play. Mother then leaves saying "bye-bye." |
| 6 | Baby alone | 3 minutes or less | Second separation episode. |
| 7 | Stranger and baby | 3 minutes or less | Continuation of second separation. Stranger enters and gears her behavior to that of the baby. |
| 8 | Mother and baby | 3 minutes | Second reunion episode. Mother enters, greets baby, then picks him up. Meanwhile stranger leaves unobtrusively. |

*Source:* Ainsworth, M. D. S., Blehar, M. C., Waters, E., & Wall, S. (1978). *Patterns of attachment: a psychological study of the strange situation* (p. 413). Hillsdale, NJ: Lawrence Erlbaum Associates, Inc. Copyright 1978 by Lawrence Erlbaum Associates, Inc. Reprinted with permission.

Another classification of attachment, described by Main and Solomon (1990) as "disorganized," suggests that disorganization or conflicted feelings and behaviors expressing stress or anxiety can occur in any of Ainsworth's three categories of attachment. This disorganization occurs frequently among children who are at risk for abuse and neglect because of maternal depression or other parental maladaptive behaviors, low socioeconomic status, and little or no intervention by social service agencies. Expressions of these disorganized attachment behaviors increase in frequency as the severity of the social risk factors increases. Some researchers believe that disorganization of attachment patterns may foretell later hostile behaviors in children (Lyons-Ruth, Alpern, & Repacholi, 1993). Avoidant attachments are also thought to predict later anti-social behaviors (Fagot & Kavanagh, 1990).

On the positive side, a large body of research found that securely attached infants:

- Formed early attachments between one and four months of age as a result of their mothers' sensitive responses to their cues
- Exhibited trust in their mothers' availability
- Progressed toward autonomous behaviors more easily
- Exhibited more confidence in exploratory behaviors
- Played with toys and other objects more than insecurely attached infants
- Enjoyed greater involvement and success in peer interactions as they got older (Cassidy & Berlin, 1994; Isabella, 1993).

What did these infants experience that their less successfully attached age-mates did not? Do certain parental characteristics facilitate the attachment process? A number of researchers suggest that the mothers (or primary care-givers) of these infants exhibited more sensitive and responsive behaviors toward them. These mothers:

- Were more involved with their infants
- Were sensitive to their infants' behavioral cues
- Were readily accessible
- Were predictable
- Responded to their infants in developmentally appropriate ways
- Generally exhibited more positive behaviors and interactions and expressions of affection
- Enjoyed close physical contact with their infants
- Encouraged exploratory play and timed their interactions strategically so as not to intrude in their infants' play
- Had a sense of when to interact (Ainsworth, Bell, & Stayton, 1974; Cassidy & Berlin, 1994; Grossmann, Grossmann, Spangler, Suess, & Unzner, 1985; Isabella, 1993; Isabella, Belsky, & von Eye, 1989).

Many scholars view the security or insecurity of the infant mother attachment as influencing the quality of all other relationships. However, Main and Weston (1981) determined that infants can form independent attachments to both mothers *and* fathers resulting from the types of interactions they have with each. Moreover, these scholars found that infants who have established secure attachments with both parents are more empathic during the toddler years to an adult in distress. Recent researchers have determined that while infants are capable of becoming closely attached to more than one caregiver, they tend to place these attachment people in an internal heirarchy or preference order (Lieberman & Zeanah, 1995). Other studies have found that when infant-mother attachments were insecure, secure infant-father attachments did not necessarily buffer the effects (Easterbrooks and Goldberg, 1990). However, this may be due to the fact that fathers in this particular study (and era) did not spend as much time with their infants and were not as engaged as the mothers in the infant's daily care routines. While Belsky and Rovine (1988) found that infants in nonmaternal care for more than 20 hours a week were at risk of developing insecure attachments with their mothers, this did not occur among infants who were cared for by their fathers in their mothers' absence. Hence, it appears that fathers can play a critical role in healthy attachment behaviors. Fike (1993) provides suggestions for both meeting fathers' needs for interaction with their children and fostering the very important relationships that develop between infants and fathers. Fathers should

1. Understand the importance of setting positive expectations for their infants and practice a mental attitude of expecting positive relationships to develop
2. Appreciate the importance of holding, cuddling, and playing with their infants
3. Become involved in the daily lives of their infants through routines such as feeding, changing, bedtime and playtime routines, and so on
4. Become aware of the day-to-day events unfolding in their infants' lives
5. Communicate verbally with their infants in tones of approval and acceptance
6. Nurture their infants through attitudes, deeds, and actions that communicate the infants' unique worth

As fathers in our society become an increasing part of their infants' and young children's lives, researchers will explore even further the positive outcomes that can accrue. Professionals will be determining how best to help fathers become more comfortable in an active role in child growth and development and their shared experiences with others who are important in their infant's lives.

Longitudinal studies have documented the long-term results of secure and insecure attachments. Many researchers have found that personality development is either positively or negatively affected by these early secure or insecure attachments. This expanding area of research has been enormously helpful to the early childhood professional by:

- Emphasizing the importance of the first year for the development of parent-child bonds
- Affirming the ameliorative potential for other attachments (family member, child care providers) when parental (or primary caregiver) attachments are insecure

- Affirming the importance of nonparental caregivers in complementing and supporting parent-child attachments
- Supporting the need for professional intervention when parent-child relationships are dysfunctional

## Social Learning Theory

Recall from Chapter 1 that behavioristic theories place considerable emphasis on external events and environmental influences in shaping children's learning and personalities. As we discuss psychosocial development in infancy, Bandura's social cognitive theory comes into play. Bandura advanced the importance of observation and imitation in human development and first illustrated his theory through his famous Bobo doll experiment (see Chapter 1). He brought into focus the importance of role models in shaping the behaviors of children. Bandura also proposed that human beings are not simply passive recipients of information and experience, but because humans have sophisticated cognitive abilities and potential, they can draw on past experiences to think about the consequences of their behavior and anticipate future possibilities for themselves. Bandura also furthered the concept of **reciprocal determinism.** As infants and children become **socialized** within their families and cultural groups, their own unique characteristics, behaviors, and levels of understanding affect the manner in which they respond to people and events in the environment. But equally influential is the fact that the unique characteristics of the infant's social environment also affect the infant. Unlike age/stage theories, social learning theory suggests that the course of development for any one individual depends on the kinds of reciprocal social learning experiences encountered. The individual's responses and interactions change over time as the individual matures and his or her realm of social experiences enlarges.

**reciprocal determinism:** a socialization process through which the individual both influences and is influenced by the environment

**socialization:** the process by which individuals acquire the accepted behaviors and values of their families and society

Bandura's perspective brings us to the concept of context in a broader sense where we must recall contextualistic theories such as Bronfrenbrenner and Gottlieb. Again the reader is referred to Chapter 1 for a description of these theories. In terms of psychosocial development of the infant, it is important to note that during the first year of life, a microsystem (Bronfrenbrenner, 1986) surrounds the child exerting primary influence through the child's home and family and through nonparental caregivers and the settings in which this occurs. As infants grow and change, their needs and capabilities change resulting in changes in both their physical and interactive environments. For instance, when infants begin to roll over and sit alone, they can be provided greater space for movement, a different array of toys than they previously experienced to support their emerging motor activity, and are more comfortable in a high chair for feeding. These abilities change appreciably the types of safety protections imposed on the infant and the types of interactions between the infant and objects and people in their environment. These supports and interactions then produce more changes in the growing infant and as circles of influence enlarge this type of reciprocal influence becomes a continuous process. The growing child affects his or her environment and the environment affects the growing child. We will not elaborate on Gottlieb's (1992) model here, but you might wish to revisit it in Chapter 5 to further explain and enlarge upon the concept of bidirectional influences on individual development.

## Social Cognition

From the foregoing, we are directed toward a discussion of how children develop understanding of behavior and behavioral expectations. **Social cognition** is the ability to understand the needs, feelings, motives, thoughts, intentions, and behaviors of oneself and others. As infants develop a basic sense of trust, they learn to associate certain behaviors that elicit certain responses from their caregivers. This awareness marks the beginning of the development of social cognition.

**social cognition:** the ability to understand the thoughts, intentions, and behaviors of oneself and others

From their experiences during the first year of life, infants become aware of the rhythms, sights, and sounds of the household (or child care setting) and the unique ways in which different adults (or siblings) hold and care for them. They learn to anticipate certain responses to their various cues; recognize the unique aromas of their mothers, fathers, and other caregivers; and perhaps sense the moods of these individuals by the manner in which they respond to them. In adult-infant interactions, the adult typically imitates the infant's facial expressions and vocalizations. As the infant experiences these pleasant interactions, the imitation becomes reciprocal, with the infant imitating the gestures, facial expressions, and vocalizations of the parent or caregivers. Infants' responses to facial expressions indicate that they look to others, usually attachment people, for clues in understanding the sights and sounds around them (Tronick, Cohn, & Shea, 1986).

Imitative behaviors become a means of both social cognition and interpersonal communication. Imitations seen in games of pat-a-cake and peek-a-boo, and in learning to kiss or wave are behaviors indicative of emerging social cognition. As the infant experiences these social events and finds them pleasurable, the desire to repeat them emerges. These and other forms of infant interpersonal communications contribute to social cognition and have implications for later language and cognitive development (Clyman, Emde, Kempe, & Harmon, 1986) as well as enhancing the social competence of the child.

# THE NEUROBIOLOGY OF PSYCHOSOCIAL DEVELOPMENT

## The Relationship of Long-Held Theories to Emerging Brain Growth Research

Revelations about early brain growth and neurological development support many of the theoretical perspectives on child development. Among them, the notion that there are periods during growth and development in which experiences seem to have greater or lesser effect on the changing organism holds sway across the spectrum from theory to hard data from the biological and neuroscientific fields. Whether we are talking about "stages" or "windows of opportunity," the concept of periods of vulnerability in which certain experiences enhance or thwart emerging development is an important one. The long-term effects of early experiences are also supported through neurobiological studies. Even though there is always time to learn new ways of thinking and behaving, the fact that neurological development is in a period of profound growth during the first three to ten years suggests the critical need for appropriate experiences. Thus, for example, the long-held theoretical perspectives on the importance of

*"Goodness of fit" between infant and the personalities and expectations of their caregivers supports psychosocial development.*

early bonding and attachments is affirmed through contemporary neurobiological discoveries. (As we will see in later chapters, numerous long-held theories now enjoy contemporary support and amplification from research in the biological sciences.) Further, while genetics remains the determinant of many traits and characteristics, the human organism remains dependent on its environment for the opportunity to develop optimally—a perspective that is reinforced through scientific data on how the human brain becomes neurologically wired.

## Psychosocial Development: A Neurological Perspective

Recall from Chapter 5 that the human organism has sophisticated capabilities for receiving and interpreting information about its internal and external environment through the sensory system. The human brain controls sensations, thinking, feeling, behaving, and emotions. It controls the expressions of joy, love, hate, friendship, curiosity, fear, sadness, shyness, anxiety, and many other responses. Throughout the early childhood years, information derived through the senses and interactions with others stimulate the growth of a complex network of neural connections as axons grow and dendrites proliferate to communicate through synaptic activity that come to control these expressions. Not only the types of earliest experiences, but the timing of experiences influences the extent to which synaptic activity occurs and results in positive growth-enhancing outcomes.

   While a great deal of genetically driven neurological development has taken place prenatally, external stimuli come importantly into play at birth and exert further influence on the formation of the brain's neurological circuitry. This neurological wiring is forming during the first three years for some developmental achievements and continues up to seven to ten years for others. Environmental sensory stimuli cause the brain to develop its own unique circuitry and influences which connections will last and which will atrophy or be pruned away for lack of use and, in some instances, which connections will be rerouted in response to injury, insult, or neglect. All of the sensory input that the child receives affects neurological development by strengthening synapses. Hence, two concepts are of critical importance in this discussion: the concept of windows of opportunity and the concept of essential experiences.

   As defined in Chapter 5, a *window of opportunity* is a period during growth and development when experiences are thought to have their greatest impact on the brain's formation of intricate neurological connections (see Figure 5.4). During these periods, there is heightened sensitivity to environmental influences. Environmental influences, then, must be carefully considered for their positive or negative effects.

   During these windows of opportunity, certain *essential experiences* strengthen specific synaptic activity. Deprivation, neglect, or abuse, while harmful at any point, can during these identified windows of opportunity have particularly long-lasting deleterious neurological effects (Perry, 1996; Perry, Polland, Blakley, Baker, & Vigilante, 1995). Essential experiences are those needed to stimulate and enhance synaptic activity during early growth and development. They are the experiences and interactions that are provided by nurturing and supportive caregivers and lead to positive outcomes for memory and learning, expression and control of emotions, and social interactive behaviors. Box 6.1 gives examples of the types of essential experiences believed to support healthy brain growth and neurological development.

   Of particular interest in our discussion of psychosocial development are the windows of opportunity for the development of social attachment (birth to age two years), and learning to control emotions, and developing the capacity to cope with stress (birth to age three years), and the essential experiences supportive of this development.

   It appears that strong secure attachment to a nurturing caregiver can provide a protective biological structure that functions to buffer an infant against the later effects of stress or trauma (Gunnar, 1996). Gunnar and her associates at the University of Minnesota studied levels of a steroid hormone known as cortisol in children's reactions to stress. Cortisol is present in saliva, and its level increases when a person experiences physiological or psychological stress or trauma. Cortisol is only one of many chemicals that function as important neurotransmitters during synaptic activity. However, elevated cortisol affects metabolism, has been associated with depression and circulatory and heart disease, can suppress the immune system, and, when chronic, can lead to destruction of neurons that are associated with learning and memory (Dienstbier, 1989; Vincent, 1990).

   Neuroscientists now caution that stressful or traumatic experiences in infancy and early childhood, when prolonged and uninterrupted by successful intervention strategies, can undermine neurological development and impair brain function. Children who suffer chronically high levels of cortisol have been shown to exhibit more developmental delays in cognitive, motor, and social

BOX 6.1    Essential Experiences in Infancy

| Development Domain | Esssential Experiences |
|---|---|
| Social attachment and the ability to cope with stress | Consistent care that is predictable, warm and nurturing. Gentle, loving, and dependable relationships with primary caregivers. Immediate attention to physiological needs for nourishment, elimination, cleanliness, warmth, exercise, and symptoms of illness. Satisfying and enjoyable social interactions, playful experiences, and engaging infant toys. |
| Regulation and control of emotions | Empathic adult responses and unconditional acceptance of the child's unique characteristics and personality traits. Adult expectations that are appropriate for the age and the individual. Guidance that is instructive and helps the child to learn about emotions and that suggests appropriate ways and contexts for the expressions of emotions. Relationships that are psychologically safe, that is free of threat, coercion, teasing, or physical or psychological neglect or abuse. Opportunities to engage in socially and emotionally satisfying play. |
| Vision and auditory acuity | Regular vision and hearing examinations by health care professionals. Interesting and varied visual and auditory fields accompanied by verbal interactions that label and describe. Personal belongings, toys, and baby books that enlist interest in color, shape, texture, size, pattern, sound, pitch, rhythm, and movement. Experience with many forms of music, song, and dance. |
| Motor development and coordination | Opportunities and encouragement to use emerging muscle coordinations in safe and interesting surroundings. Supportive and positive interactions for effort. Play space, equipment, and toys that facilitate both large and small motor coordinations. |
| Vocabulary and language development | Rich verbal interactions that respond to the infant's efforts to communicate. Engaging the infant in talking, chanting, singing, sharing, picture books, telling stories, and sharing poems and rhymes. Toys and props that encourage pretend play. Conversations characterized by varied topics, interesting vocabulary, engaging facial expressions and voice inflections. Interesting and enlightening firsthand experiences. Focused and responsive interactions in both native and second languages. Opportunities to converse and sing in either language. |
| Cognitive development | Toys and learning materials that encourage manipulations and constructions, dumping and pouring, pushing and pulling, dropping and retrieving, hiding and finding. Toys and props that encourage and support pretend play. Social interactions that facilitate explorations and play. Baby books that introduce familiar objects, labels, and simple stories. Selected recorded music, or pleasing instrumental music and singing. |

development than other children (Gunnar, 1996). Earliest nurturing experiences and strong parent-child bonds during the first year appear to build inner strength (both biological and psychological) against the deleterious effects of stress and trauma, a strength that remains evident as children get older. School-age children who have enjoyed secure attachment dynamics during infancy and early childhood exhibit fewer behavior problems when stress or trauma confronts them.

Further, it is believed that the ability to express and control emotions has biological origins derived from the types of care, nurturing, and supportive interactions that stimulate specific neurological connections (Perry, 1996; Perry, Polland, Blakley, Baker, & Vigilante, 1995). Early experiences quite literally shape the biological systems (neurological "wiring" and chemical characteristics) that underly expressions of emotions. Children who have been abused, abandoned, neglected, and otherwise emotionally maltreated suffer impaired ability to regulate their emotional responses due to abnormal migrations of neurons and synaptic activity (Perry, 1996; Perry et al., 1995). As we learn more about the timing and intensity of these insults to brain growth and neurological development, we will be better able to identify risk factors and to develop timely intervention strategies that prevent or correct the effects of injurious environments and enhance subsequent developmental outcomes (Puckett, Marshall, & Davis, 1999).

# DIMENSIONS OF PSYCHOSOCIAL DEVELOPMENT IN INFANCY

## Infant Temperament

From birth, infants display distinctive personality characteristics, the study of which has intrigued parents and researchers alike. Quite often, discussions of personality center on temperament, a characteristic that is believed to be at least in part influenced by genetic endowment (Plomin, 1987). Researchers have focused variously on dimensions of temperament, such as emotionality (the extent to which events can be upsetting), activity (types and pace of behaviors), and sociability (the desire for social proximity and interaction versus shyness or withdrawal) (Buss & Plomin, 1984; Kagan, Reznick & Snidman, 1988; Kagan, Snidman, & Arcus, 1992). In studying individuality in children, Stella Chess and Alexander Thomas (1987) identified a number of dimensions of behavior that are associated with temperament. The components of temperament that they studied include activity level, rhythmicity (regularity or predictability of biological functions such as wake/sleep patterns and eating), approach and withdrawal behaviors, adaptability, sensory threshold, intensity of response, quality of mood, distractability, persistence, and attention span. By gathering information about these behaviors in large numbers of children, Chess and Thomas were able to delineate three main types of temperament:

1. *The easy temperament.* The child is usually easygoing, even-tempered, tolerant of change, playful, responsive, and adaptable. The child eats and sleeps with some regularity, is easily comforted when upset, and generally displays a positive mood.

2. *The difficult temperament.* The child is slower to develop regular eating and sleeping routines, is more irritable, derives less pleasure from playtime activities, has difficulty adjusting to changes in routines, and tends to cry louder and longer than more easily soothed children.

3. *The slow-to-warm-up temperament.* The child displays only mild positive or negative reactions, resists new situations and people, and is moody and slow to adapt. The slow-to-warm-up child may resist close interactions such as cuddling.

The easy child's behaviors provide positive feedback and reinforcement to caregivers and, in so doing, influence the kinds and amounts of attention the child will receive throughout early development. More often than not, these children experience what Chess and Thomas (1987) have called a "goodness of fit" between themselves and the personalities and expectations of their caregivers. *Goodness of fit* is defined as a principle of interaction in which

> the organism's capacities, motivations and styles of behaving and the demands and expectations of the environment are in accord. Such consonance between organism and environment potentiates optimal positive development. Should there be dissonance between the capacities and characteristics of the organism on the one hand and the environment opportunities and demands on the other hand, there is poorness of fit, which leads to maladaptive functioning and distorted development. (Chess & Thomas, 1987, pp. 20–21)

Infants who are described as temperamentally difficult may fail to elicit appropriate nurturing and support from their caregivers. Adults who find this temperament hard to respond to may become punitive, overly demanding, or perhaps inconsistent and appeasing in their interactions. They may be vague or unclear with their child about their expectations, or perhaps, their acceptance of them. The adults themselves may feel inadequate to their task, helpless, and confused. Poorly prepared to deal with a difficult temperament, these adults may engage in power struggles for control. Obviously a "poorness of fit" emerges in these situations and holds potential for ineffective and negative relationships and childhood behavior disorders that can persist into adulthood.

The slow-to-warm-up child generally does not present substantial difficulties in the adult-child relationship. However, this child, being slower to adapt and reticent with new acquaintances and situations, may not receive persistent efforts on the part of caregivers to maintain positive interactions.

Not all children fall neatly into these categories; easy children are not always easy, difficult children are not always difficult, and slow-to-warm-up children are not always reticent. However, these descriptions help us to appreciate wide variations in infant and child personalities. Recognizing and appreciating individual differences helps adults to respond appropriately to these behaviors. Adults must be cautious in applying these categories, however. Self-fulfilling prophecies may occur in which the child behaves according to adult expectations. If adults ascribe labels and misunderstand the infant's cues, they may fail to support the infant's needs for positive and nurturing interactions, regardless of temperament or personality type. If there is goodness of fit between infants and their environments, there are positive outcomes that carry over into later development.

2. *The difficult temperament.* The child is slower to develop regular eating and sleeping routines, is more irritable, derives less pleasure from playtime activities, has difficulty adjusting to changes in routines, and tends to cry louder and longer than more easily soothed children.

3. *The slow-to-warm-up temperament.* The child displays only mild positive or negative reactions, resists new situations and people, and is moody and slow to adapt. The slow-to-warm-up child may resist close interactions such as cuddling.

The easy child's behaviors provide positive feedback and reinforcement to caregivers and, in so doing, influence the kinds and amounts of attention the child will receive throughout early development. More often than not, these children experience what Chess and Thomas (1987) have called a "goodness of fit" between themselves and the personalities and expectations of their caregivers. *Goodness of fit* is defined as a principle of interaction in which

> the organism's capacities, motivations and styles of behaving and the demands and expectations of the environment are in accord. Such consonance between organism and environment potentiates optimal positive development. Should there be dissonance between the capacities and characteristics of the organism on the one hand and the environment opportunities and demands on the other hand, there is poorness of fit, which leads to maladaptive functioning and distorted development. (Chess & Thomas, 1987, pp. 20–21)

Infants who are described as temperamentally difficult may fail to elicit appropriate nurturing and support from their caregivers. Adults who find this temperament hard to respond to may become punitive, overly demanding, or perhaps inconsistent and appeasing in their interactions. They may be vague or unclear with their child about their expectations, or perhaps, their acceptance of them. The adults themselves may feel inadequate to their task, helpless, and confused. Poorly prepared to deal with a difficult temperament, these adults may engage in power struggles for control. Obviously a "poorness of fit" emerges in these situations and holds potential for ineffective and negative relationships and childhood behavior disorders that can persist into adulthood.

The slow-to-warm-up child generally does not present substantial difficulties in the adult-child relationship. However, this child, being slower to adapt and reticent with new acquaintances and situations, may not receive persistent efforts on the part of caregivers to maintain positive interactions.

Not all children fall neatly into these categories; easy children are not always easy, difficult children are not always difficult, and slow-to-warm-up children are not always reticent. However, these descriptions help us to appreciate wide variations in infant and child personalities. Recognizing and appreciating individual differences helps adults to respond appropriately to these behaviors. Adults must be cautious in applying these categories, however. Self-fulfilling prophecies may occur in which the child behaves according to adult expectations. If adults ascribe labels and misunderstand the infant's cues, they may fail to support the infant's needs for positive and nurturing interactions, regardless of temperament or personality type. If there is goodness of fit between infants and their environments, there are positive outcomes that carry over into later development.

While a great deal of genetically driven neurological development has taken place prenatally, external stimuli come importantly into play at birth and exert further influence on the formation of the brain's neurological circuitry. This neurological wiring is forming during the first three years for some developmental achievements and continues up to seven to ten years for others. Environmental sensory stimuli cause the brain to develop its own unique circuitry and influences which connections will last and which will atrophy or be pruned away for lack of use and, in some instances, which connections will be rerouted in response to injury, insult, or neglect. All of the sensory input that the child receives affects neurological development by strengthening synapses. Hence, two concepts are of critical importance in this discussion: the concept of windows of opportunity and the concept of essential experiences.

As defined in Chapter 5, a *window of opportunity* is a period during growth and development when experiences are thought to have their greatest impact on the brain's formation of intricate neurological connections (see Figure 5.4). During these periods, there is heightened sensitivity to environmental influences. Environmental influences, then, must be carefully considered for their positive or negative effects.

During these windows of opportunity, certain *essential experiences* strengthen specific synaptic activity. Deprivation, neglect, or abuse, while harmful at any point, can during these identified windows of opportunity have particularly long-lasting deleterious neurological effects (Perry, 1996; Perry, Polland, Blakley, Baker, & Vigilante, 1995). Essential experiences are those needed to stimulate and enhance synaptic activity during early growth and development. They are the experiences and interactions that are provided by nurturing and supportive caregivers and lead to positive outcomes for memory and learning, expression and control of emotions, and social interactive behaviors. Box 6.1 gives examples of the types of essential experiences believed to support healthy brain growth and neurological development.

Of particular interest in our discussion of psychosocial development are the windows of opportunity for the development of social attachment (birth to age two years), and learning to control emotions, and developing the capacity to cope with stress (birth to age three years), and the essential experiences supportive of this development.

It appears that strong secure attachment to a nurturing caregiver can provide a protective biological structure that functions to buffer an infant against the later effects of stress or trauma (Gunnar, 1996). Gunnar and her associates at the University of Minnesota studied levels of a steroid hormone known as cortisol in children's reactions to stress. Cortisol is present in saliva, and its level increases when a person experiences physiological or psychological stress or trauma. Cortisol is only one of many chemicals that function as important neurotransmitters during synaptic activity. However, elevated cortisol affects metabolism, has been associated with depression and circulatory and heart disease, can suppress the immune system, and, when chronic, can lead to destruction of neurons that are associated with learning and memory (Dienstbier, 1989; Vincent, 1990).

Neuroscientists now caution that stressful or traumatic experiences in infancy and early childhood, when prolonged and uninterrupted by successful intervention strategies, can undermine neurological development and impair brain function. Children who suffer chronically high levels of cortisol have been shown to exhibit more developmental delays in cognitive, motor, and social

## BOX 6.1   Essential Experiences in Infancy

| Development Domain | Esssential Experiences |
|---|---|
| Social attachment and the ability to cope with stress | Consistent care that is predictable, warm and nurturing. Gentle, loving, and dependable relationships with primary caregivers. Immediate attention to physiological needs for nourishment, elimination, cleanliness, warmth, exercise, and symptoms of illness. Satisfying and enjoyable social interactions, playful experiences, and engaging infant toys. |
| Regulation and control of emotions | Empathic adult responses and unconditional acceptance of the child's unique characteristics and personality traits. Adult expectations that are appropriate for the age and the individual. Guidance that is instructive and helps the child to learn about emotions and that suggests appropriate ways and contexts for the expressions of emotions. Relationships that are psychologically safe, that is free of threat, coercion, teasing, or physical or psychological neglect or abuse. Opportunities to engage in socially and emotionally satisfying play. |
| Vision and auditory acuity | Regular vision and hearing examinations by health care professionals. Interesting and varied visual and auditory fields accompanied by verbal interactions that label and describe. Personal belongings, toys, and baby books that enlist interest in color, shape, texture, size, pattern, sound, pitch, rhythm, and movement. Experience with many forms of music, song, and dance. |
| Motor development and coordination | Opportunities and encouragement to use emerging muscle coordinations in safe and interesting surroundings. Supportive and positive interactions for effort. Play space, equipment, and toys that facilitate both large and small motor coordinations. |
| Vocabulary and language development | Rich verbal interactions that respond to the infant's efforts to communicate. Engaging the infant in talking, chanting, singing, sharing, picture books, telling stories, and sharing poems and rhymes. Toys and props that encourage pretend play. Conversations characterized by varied topics, interesting vocabulary, engaging facial expressions and voice inflections. Interesting and enlightening firsthand experiences. Focused and responsive interactions in both native and second languages. Opportunities to converse and sing in either language. |
| Cognitive development | Toys and learning materials that encourage manipulations and constructions, dumping and pouring, pushing and pulling, dropping and retrieving, hiding and finding. Toys and props that encourage and support pretend play. Social interactions that facilitate explorations and play. Baby books that introduce familiar objects, labels, and simple stories. Selected recorded music, or pleasing instrumental music and singing. |

development than other children (Gunnar, 1996). Earliest nurturing experiences and strong parent-child bonds during the first year appear to build inner strength (both biological and psychological) against the deleterious effects of stress and trauma, a strength that remains evident as children get older. School-age children who have enjoyed secure attachment dynamics during infancy and early childhood exhibit fewer behavior problems when stress or trauma confronts them.

Further, it is believed that the ability to express and control emotions has biological origins derived from the types of care, nurturing, and supportive interactions that stimulate specific neurological connections (Perry, 1996; Perry, Polland, Blakley, Baker, & Vigilante, 1995). Early experiences quite literally shape the biological systems (neurological "wiring" and chemical characteristics) that underly expressions of emotions. Children who have been abused, abandoned, neglected, and otherwise emotionally maltreated suffer impaired ability to regulate their emotional responses due to abnormal migrations of neurons and synaptic activity (Perry, 1996; Perry et al., 1995). As we learn more about the timing and intensity of these insults to brain growth and neurological development, we will be better able to identify risk factors and to develop timely intervention strategies that prevent or correct the effects of injurious environments and enhance subsequent developmental outcomes (Puckett, Marshall, & Davis, 1999).

## DIMENSIONS OF PSYCHOSOCIAL DEVELOPMENT IN INFANCY

### Infant Temperament

From birth, infants display distinctive personality characteristics, the study of which has intrigued parents and researchers alike. Quite often, discussions of personality center on temperament, a characteristic that is believed to be at least in part influenced by genetic endowment (Plomin, 1987). Researchers have focused variously on dimensions of temperament, such as emotionality (the extent to which events can be upsetting), activity (types and pace of behaviors), and sociability (the desire for social proximity and interaction versus shyness or withdrawal) (Buss & Plomin, 1984; Kagan, Reznick & Snidman, 1988; Kagan, Snidman, & Arcus, 1992). In studying individuality in children, Stella Chess and Alexander Thomas (1987) identified a number of dimensions of behavior that are associated with temperament. The components of temperament that they studied include activity level, rhythmicity (regularity or predictability of biological functions such as wake/sleep patterns and eating), approach and withdrawal behaviors, adaptability, sensory threshold, intensity of response, quality of mood, distractability, persistence, and attention span. By gathering information about these behaviors in large numbers of children, Chess and Thomas were able to delineate three main types of temperament:

1. *The easy temperament.* The child is usually easygoing, even-tempered, tolerant of change, playful, responsive, and adaptable. The child eats and sleeps with some regularity, is easily comforted when upset, and generally displays a positive mood.

## Infant Emotions

The infant displays an array of emotions, including affection, joy, surprise, anger, fear, disgust, interest, and even sadness (Campos Barrett, Lamb, Goldsmith, & Sternberg, 1983). The newborn shows interest and surprise when something catches her or his attention (T. M. Field, 1982). The newborn smiles at a pleasing sound or when hunger has been satisfied. A sudden jolt or loud noise may evoke surprise and distress. The infant may show anger or even rage at being restrained or uncomfortable.

A number of scholars have suggested sequences for the emergence of discrete emotions (e.g., Greenspan & Greenspan, 1985; Izard & Buechler, 1986; Stroufe, 1979). For instance, it is believed that distress, disgust, and surprise are expressed by newborns, while anger and joy emerge during the first four months and fear and shyness emerge between age six months and one year.

While most emotions seem to be present from birth (Campos et al., 1983), differences in emotional responses occur as the infant gets older. The most significant changes in emotional and social responses in infants occur during the period from 6 to 12 months, owing primarily to significant emerging cognitive development. The abilities to recall the past, sense discrepancies, and attend to expressions of emotion in caregivers contribute to these differences (Lamb, Morrison, & Malkin, 1987). Thus, the emergence of fear of strangers and separation anxiety described earlier is further explained.

## Crying: An Essential Mode of Communication

Infants are competent communicators first communicating their needs through crying. The first infant cries are reflexive, perhaps survival reactions to physiological needs for nourishment, warmth, movement, touch, or relief from discomfort. Infants have no control over their crying and will not be able to stop crying until a need has been met or they have exhausted themselves. As the infant gets older, the causes of crying change from internal to external stimuli and may be provoked by such things as loud noises, physical restraint, uncomfortable clothing, frustration with toys, or, as described earlier in this chapter, fear of strangers and of separation.

Infant crying frequently has different tones, rhythms, and intensities. Parents soon learn the nature and the message of their infant's various cries and respond according to various acoustical differences (Green, Jones, & Gustafson, 1987). Shaffer (1971) identified three distinct patterns of crying: the basic cry usually associated with hunger, an angry cry, and a pain cry.

Crying is sometimes unsettling to parents and caregivers, particularly when they are unable to determine the infant's needs. Learning to distinguish the accoustical variations in an infant's cries and what each means is one of the tasks of parenting and infant caregiving. Bell and Ainsworth (1972) found that infants whose parents responded promptly to their cries and other signals cried less often. When the infants did cry, the crying was of shorter duration. Further, infants who cried and fussed the most after three months of age were the ones whose parents did not respond readily to their cries. Another study found that infants who were held and carried about during the day cried less during the night (Hunziker & Barr, 1986).

As with older children and adults, infants experience boredom, loneliness, and a need for personal contact. Sometimes crying simply signals a need for companionship, the sound of a familiar voice, and the sensation of a familiar touch. When bored, infants may cry for a change of position or place or for the nearness and interaction of others. Certain music or recorded soothing sounds or perhaps selected visual stimuli that engage the child's attention may help to meet the child's needs. Brazelton describes infant nursing behaviors as having feeding bursts and pauses in which the pause appears to be intentional to capture social stimuli (Brazelton, 1992). He emphasizes the importance of interaction, talking and quietly playing with an infant during feeding time. On the other hand, when infants are difficult to console, adults must find the just right interaction to comfort. Rocking the infant; holding the infant to one's shoulder to provide opportunities for visual scanning; talking in soft, soothing tones; gentle caresses; and directing the infant's attention to objects, toys, and other children are usually successful ways to calm a fussy infant.

## Other Modes of Infant Communication

Parents and other caregivers who are cognizant of the infant's various means of communicating, such as whimpering, facial expressions, wiggling, vocalizing, and turning away from stimuli, are better able to respond and interact appropriately with their infants. These adults take cues from infant behaviors recognizing signals of contentment, discomfort, distress, or frustration. Infants whose caregivers respond to these noncrying signals soon learn to communicate without crying, unless, of course, there is pain, fear, frustration, or exhaustion. These infants will grow in their sense of trust in their caregivers and in themselves as communicators.

 *Cheryl's mother* finds it difficult to work as a housekeeper and help to care for Angela. Cheryl goes to school and feels pressured to find other child care arrangements. The older siblings in the family have been called on to help with baby-sitting, but that has not always worked out, owing to their own childhood needs for play and socialization and desires to succeed in school.

James has tried to be helpful, but his visits to his infant daughter are becoming less and less frequent. His own need to work and his desire to stay in school consume his time and energies. His feelings for both Cheryl and their baby are becoming ambivalent and confused, and he sometimes feels depressed. He isn't sure what his role should be.

Cheryl has experienced mixed feelings as the realities of constantly having to meet an infant's needs become more apparent. She isn't sure of James anymore and anticipates that they will probably split up soon. She feels sad, though she does not blame him. She is tired most of the time, since she has returned to school and her classes have become quite demanding. Sometimes she feels like a failure at school and at mothering, and her baby seems cranky much of the time.

Cheryl's mother frequently shares her frustrations with a friend at her church, including the difficulties of making a living and raising a two-generation family. Her friend tells her that some high schools in the area provide on-site child care for teenage mothers. Through a number of inquiries, Cheryl's mother is able to identify one such high school. It isn't the high school in which Cheryl is currently enrolled and will necessitate a family move if Cheryl chooses to take advantage of the child care program.

After several weeks of searching, Cheryl's family locates a small house within walking distance of the new high school. Cheryl doesn't want to move, yet she feels that she has no choice. She will miss James and her other friends. James offers to help; he will borrow his brother's pickup truck and will help them to prepare the new house for occupancy. Cheryl is pleased at this show of caring and thinks that maybe her relationship with James can continue.

Meanwhile, Angela has experienced a constant turnover in caregivers. At age eight months, her sleeping patterns are still irregular and unpredictable. She is hungry at odd hours and is a finicky eater. She cries easily and often, continuously demands the company of others, and vigorously resists being put to bed. She can be quite playful, however, and enjoys the attention of her school-age aunts and uncles. She responds readily to Cheryl, but her relationship with her grandmother seems more comforting. She watches the comings and goings of all the family members and frets or cries when left in her playpen as others leave the room. Both Cheryl and her mother care deeply for Angela and want her to be a happy, cheerful baby.

*Jeremy's experiences* have been quite different. His psychosocial world has included his mother, his father, Phyllis (his baby-sitter), and an occasional visit from grandparents and trips to the church nursery. Except for his bouts with colic, Jeremy's routines of sleeping and eating are generally without incident. Bathing, dressing, playing, and interacting with Phyllis and his parents are, for the most part, relaxed, predictable, and enjoyable.

Ann, now back at work, is making every effort to maintain a sense of order in their lives, though meeting Jeremy's needs has at times overwhelmed her. Ann and Bill talk frequently and frankly about the dramatic change in their lifestyle, daily schedules, social life, and physical stamina.

Bill feels a need and a desire to nurture Jeremy and misses the child when he is at work. Jeremy has become his "buddy," and Bill cherishes the smiles, the reaching toward Daddy's face when being held, and the pounding at his legs with uncoordinated hands to get attention or to be held. Dinnertimes are not always serene, nor are bedtimes, yet Bill and Ann both savor the changes they are observing in their growing baby. Indeed, Jeremy has a distinct personality. Does he take after Bill's side of the family or Ann's? Together, they anticipate Jeremy's changing looks, behaviors, and interactions with each of them.

Since Jeremy's routines have been mostly predictable and pleasurable, with the adults in his world responding to his cues in focused ways, his sense of trust is emerging, and he has learned which cues result in which responses from others. At eight months, however, he is beginning to fret on separation from his parents and sometimes from Phyliis. He is especially wary of strangers and seems to need more close physical contact than usual. He also cries more frequently than he used to and is especially difficult in the mornings when Ann and Bill are scurrying to dress and leave for work.

## Self-Awareness

It is believed that to become a participant in the give-and-take of a relationship, the infant must first develop a sense of self as distinct and apart from others (M. Lewis, 1987; M. Lewis, & Brooks-Gunn, 1979). Emotions such as love, hate, jealousy, and guilt—the types of complex emotions that are evoked through relationships with others—are related to an individual's sense of self. Five periods in the development of self-other differentiation have been identified by Lewis (1987):

Period 1 (0–3 months) is characterized by reflexive interactions between the infant and caregivers and objects.

Period 2 (3–8 months) is a period in which the infant, through increasing numbers of experiences with others, progresses toward greater distinction between self and others, though the child may not make these distinctions in all situations. Period 3 (8–12 months) is a period in which self-other differentiation appears to be accomplished; the infant evidences awareness of self as different and permanent in time and space.

Period 4 (12–18 months) is a period in which self-conscious emotions such as embarrassment and separation anxiety begin to emerge, as does the ability to recognize oneself in mirror or photo images.

Period 5 (18–30 months) is a period in which self-definition begins to emerge in which the infant can refer through language to age, gender, and other defining characteristics.

The emergence of self-awareness depends on cognitive development—the ability to make mental "like me"/"not like me" distinctions. Self-awareness is also dependent on social experiences. Infants develop their understanding of self and subsequently a self-concept through their social interactive experiences with others: how others respond to them. As we will see in later chapters, self-concepts are continually being modified as new abilities emerge and social interactions expand beyond primary caregivers.

## Social Smiling and Facial Expressions

Smiles observed in the neonate are thought to be triggered by internal stimuli associated with the immature central nervous system. There seems to be a developmental pattern for smiling (Campos & Stenberg, 1981; Emde & Harmon, 1972) that proceeds from internal stimuli to external elicitations.

At first, infants smile at faces regardless of facial expression. Then, from three to seven months, they begin to notice and respond to differences in facial expressions. In the latter part of the first year, infants not only can discriminate differences in facial expressions, but also may respond to each expression in a different emotional way (Campos & Stenberg, 1981). Researchers have also determined that infants from birth are capable of producing almost all of the muscle movements involved in facial expressions that display basic emotions (Oster & Ekman, 1977) and that emotions such as sadness, anger, fear, joy, interest, surprise and disgust can be observed in facial expressions of infants as early as one month of age (Izard, Huebner, Risser, McGinness, & Dougherty 1980). Whether or not these outward observable expressions can be linked conclusively to internal states or feelings is still unclear.

Infants have also been shown to respond to positive and negative affect in the human voice, smiling more to sounds of approval than to sounds of disapproval (Fernald, 1993), and to information in facial and bodily cues of their

*Infants' behavior styles influence reciprocal interactions between infants and parents and other caregivers.*

caregivers (Klinnert, Campos, Sorce, Emde, & Svejda, 1983). By six to eight months, infants use a process referred to as **social referencing** whereby they observe their familiar caregivers for affective cues to comfort or guide them in unfamiliar of frightening situations (Klinnert, et al., 1983). As infants get older, they become more skilled at social referencing, looking to parents or caregivers more quickly, more frequently, and more intently, then using these affective cues to guide their own behaviors.

social referencing: a behavior in which the emotional/social reactions of others are observed and used to guide one's own behavior in unfamiliar situations

True social smiling is thought to occur at approximately six to eight weeks. It is believed that when the infant can remember and recognize the face and perhaps the voice of the primary caregiver, smiling becomes more social (J. Kagan, 1971; Wolff, 1963). As infants get older, they become more discerning in their smiling behavior, choosing to smile at familiar faces, voices, and interactions over unfamiliar ones. Yet the frequency of smiling increases with age. Cognition seems to play a major role in the emergence of smiling that is triggered by external stimuli.

## Infant Interaction Patterns and Play Behaviors

In the first few weeks of life, the neonate's interaction patterns relate primarily to survival needs, signaling those needs to parents and caregivers through crying, squirming, and fretting. As the infant becomes more alert and begins to study the faces and responses of parents and to distinguish their primary caregivers from others, the infant's responsiveness increases. As experiences with others expand during the first year to include siblings, grandparents, nonparental caregivers, and in some cases other infants and young children, interactive strategies emerge and become more complex.

Infants' efforts to interact are characterized by gazing for some time at a face, reaching toward it, imitating facial expressions, and visually and auditorially tracking a person. Socially, the infant enjoys being gently tickled and jostled; responses include cooing, gurgling, babbling, kicking, and wiggling. Such behaviors elicit playfulness, attention, and encouragement from others.

Around age five months, interest in other children and siblings increases. The infant engages in prolonged onlooker behavior when placed in the same room with other children. Some consider this to be an early stage of social play development. Observing others is entertaining in and of itself, and infants derive considerable pleasure from simply being near the action.

Interest in siblings is particularly profound during the latter half of the first year. It is generally thought that playful and responsive siblings increase infant sociability. Some scholars believe that the infant's sociability itself influences the amount of attention received from siblings (Lamb, 1978). Regardless, infants can be extremely interested in their siblings, following them around, imitating them, actively seeking their attention, and exploring their toys and other belongings. Siblings can be taught to respond to the infant in gentle and playful ways. Around six to eight months, the infant will participate in games such as peek-a-boo and pat-a-cake and infant-initiated reciprocal activities, such as repeatedly dropping a toy to be retrieved, handed back to the infant, and dropped again.

How infants respond to other infants has been the focus of a number of studies (Adamson & Bakeman, 1985; T. M. Field, 1979; Fogel, 1979; Hay, Nash, & Petersen, 1983). Infants will react to the sound of another infant's cry and show an awareness of the presence of another infant. At six months of age, the infant will reach toward another infant, watch intently, and perhaps smile and make friendly sounds. At this age, infants have been shown to respond positively to one another in groups of two and generally to find other infants intriguing. An infant may crawl into or fall on another infant in clumsy efforts to interact; yet infant-infant interaction is seen to be positive despite its awkwardness.

## FACTORS INFLUENCING PSYCHOSOCIAL DEVELOPMENT IN INFANTS

From the foregoing, we are now able to list a number of factors that influence psychosocial development during infancy. They include the following.

### The Quality and Consistency of Care

Among the most important qualities of infant care in terms of healthy psychosocial development are *consistency, predictability,* and *continuity* of care. Though personalities and adult responses to infants vary greatly, infants need their different caregivers (mother, father, siblings, nonparent caregivers) to respond to their cues in relatively similar and nurturing ways. Also, the infant needs to trust that certain events will occur in reasonable order and with some predictability. Earliest experiences that are marked by predictability of routines, hunger satisfaction, comforting closeness, and reliable and prompt response to bids for attention and expression of need build a sense of trust that is critical to healthy psychosocial development.

## Success and Quality of Bonding and Attachments

Success and quality of attachment behaviors have been shown to affect the manner in which the brain processes social and emotional information and becomes wired for positive affect. This has long-term implications for social and emotional development and the development of social and moral competence during later childhood.

## Essential Experiences

Essential experiences occurring during opportune periods of brain growth and neurological development are simple, inexpensive, and usually come naturally but can be enhanced through conscientious effort on the part of infant caregivers. Early experiences that promote optimal early brain growth and neurological development establish a biological buffer against later stresses and enhance the ability to learn.

## Sociocultural Experiences and Relationships with Others in the Microsystem

Since the first sphere of influence on child growth and development occurs within the microsystem that includes the infant, family, and other caregivers, the child's cultural heritage comes strongly into play.

Cultural contexts influence psychosocial development through the perceptions, values, goals, and expectations associated with child rearing held by the child's particular cultural group. Expressions of emotions, expectations and encouragement of infant responses; tolerance for infant behaviors, and perceived parental roles vary among and within cultures. Attitudes toward feeding, crying, holding, and clothing, the nature and amount of language to which the infant is exposed, and attitudes toward sickness and health, medicine and social services, religious belief systems, and many other issues provide the cultural contexts through which infant psychosocial development emerges (Garcia-Coll, 1990).

Socioeconomic status also plays a role in the family dynamics surrounding children and child rearing. Of particular concern are families of very low socioeconomic means. For some (though certainly not all) families of low socioeconomic status (SES), survival needs often supersede the social and emotional needs of children and the physiological needs for food and medication. The difficulties of surviving may be so overwhelming that they interfere with healthy parent-parent and parent-child interactions. Children in such families may be hungry and/or cold, suffer more illnesses, and even be neglected or abused. Parental efforts to provide food, clothing, shelter, and transportation for the family may be thwarted. Attending to the psychosocial needs of children is precluded by fatigue, frustration, anxiety, and sometimes resentment or a sense of futility. Personality development of infants in these situations can be at risk.

For such families, high-quality child care can provide a much needed support system. The professionals involved may provide access to needed social and health care services, job counseling, and parenting education. Along with a full day of good-quality nurturing and psychosocially sound interactions, the infant is given an improved chance at healthy development. The relief from the stress associated with child rearing and the assurance that the infant is well cared for during a number of hours of the day (or night) should provide some relief for the parents in these potentially unhealthy situations.

Within the child's microsystem the integrity of all of the entities within that system is important. Family health and freedom from discord or dysfunction, economic security, and overall psychological and social well-being are important contributors to psychosocial development and its manifestation in later years.

## Interactions That Promote Social Cognition

Social interactions that provide opportunities to observe, imitate, and reference positive and supportive behaviors of others in their family and cultural groups help infants to develop social cognition. Learning to read facial expressions, body language, and other cues in their social interactions helps infants to begin to notice and regulate their own feelings and behaviors. Positive and supportive social interactions with others promote self-awareness and positive feelings.

## Goodness of Fit with Caregivers

The child's own personality, which includes characteristic temperament, influences the frequency and types of interactions with others that the child receives. The extent to which adults who care for infants can respond appropriately to different temperament profiles determines the extent to which there can be goodness-of-fit between infant and caregiver leading to positive personality outcomes. Since temperament is genetically influenced to some extent, it falls on the adult to make appropriate adaptations to the infant's expressions of need, while encouraging and modeling socially acceptable behaviors and providing unconditional acceptance of the child's uniqueness.

## Continuity of Care

Continuity of care refers to caregivers' developmental expectations for the infant and knowledge and acceptance of the infant's individual temperament, rhythms, interaction patterns, and other characteristics that make the infant unique. While many infants today are cared for by nonparental caregivers during their parents' working hours, continuity is maintained when the infant experiences a minimum number of caregivers during the course of a day or a week. Many child care centers today provide a primary caregiver to infants in an effort to reduce the number of adults to whom the infant must adapt. This practice enhances the infant's sense of order and facilitates opportunities to form positive relationships and, perhaps, healthy attachments between infant and nonparental caregivers.

The vignettes about Angela and Jeremy earlier in this chapter reveal two very different situations in the quality and consistency of care each infant is receiving. Angela's routines are less predictable; so are her caregivers, as they change frequently. The quality of care she is receiving is not optimal, and the opportunity for her to develop stable, trusting relationships is tenuous.

Jeremy, on the other hand, is experiencing daily schedules and routines that are neither rigid nor inflexible yet are predictable to him. His caregivers are limited in number, and each responds effectively to his cues for attention and other needs. In both cases, the infants are being provided with nonparental care while their parents are away at school or work. What is the relationship between nonparental care and optimal psychosocial development in infants?

## Nonparental Child Care

Today, an increasing number of infants are receiving nonparental child care. Many enter nonparental child care arrangements as early as six weeks of age. These arrangements include care by a member of the child's extended family (grandparent, aunt, uncle, cousin, older sibling), neighbor, in-home baby-sitter, family day home, and child care centers. The quality of infant care programs is always a major concern, and parents need to be discerning in their choices of individuals who will care for their infants.

Recent studies have noted varying adjustment patterns among infants receiving nonparental child care. One study noted that initially, infants showed inhibited behaviors and less positive affect similar to those expected of older children challenged by a new environment. These behaviors, however, were found to diminish over the next six months, after which the children showed more positive affect and positive peer interactions later on (Fein, Gariboldi, & Boni, 1993). This study also found that caregivers were most responsive and comforting to infants at entry and that over the next six months, the infants' distress behavior diminished. This study also suggests that it takes three to six months for infants to feel comfortable in child care settings. We can assume that with poor-quality care, the adjustment period could well be longer. However, we would not wish to wait six months to determine infants' adjustment if there is any reason to believe the care is less than optimal.

While some studies propose that long hours (20 or more) in nonparental child care can impede the development of secure attachments between infants and their mothers (Belsky, 1988; Belsky & Rovine, 1988), other studies do not support this perspective. One study (Burchinal, Bryant, Lee, & Ramey, 1992) found that nonmaternal care had no detrimental effects on the development and maintenance of infant-mother attachments at age one year if the age of entry was under seven months, before attachment patterns begin to emerge, and the quality of the child care arrangement was exemplary. This study also noted that children who received extensive nonmaternal care beginning in early infancy were as likely to develop normal infant-mother attachments as their home-raised peers were. The important point here is the quality of the child care arrangement. Quality of infant care programs is usually defined in terms of involved and developmentally appropriate caregiving, low infant to caregiver/teacher ratios, and small groups (the younger the child, the smaller the group should be).

Earlier in this chapter, we discussed the importance of the mother's and father's sensitivity and responsiveness to their infant's signals. It follows that the infant's nonparental caregivers must also be sensitive and responsive. Stressing the importance of high-quality child care programs, Raikes (1993) focused on how the amount of time an infant spends in the care of a "high-ability" teacher affects infant-teacher attachment. Since a secure attachment with a caring and nurturing caregiver can buffer the stress of parental separation, such an attachment can prove to be quite important. It is also thought that such child-caregiver attachments may even compensate for insecure parental attachments. Raikes's study was based on the following premises:

- High-ability caregivers/teachers support and facilitate the infant's developing sense of trust, predictability, and control.
- Experience with infants allows teachers to become fully acquainted with infants' personalities, that is, what upsets, excites, amuses, and bores infants.
- History in a relationship is required for secure attachments to develop.
- Infants' cognitive, social, emotional, and language development depend on quality relationships.

Raikes found that at least nine months with the same caregiver/teacher provide the best opportunity for the infant to form a secure attachment. She proposes that rather than "promoting" infants at age six or seven months, as is quite common in child care programs, a "new standard for excellence" in the field would keep infants and high-ability teachers together beyond one year of age.

Communication between parents and caregivers is also important in nonparental child care. The National Association for the Education of Young Children accreditation standards (Bredekamp, 1991) and other standards set by funding entitles encourage frequent interactions and mutual support. The amount of parent-caregiver interactions varies appreciably among child care settings, yet frequent and meaningful communication is predictive of the quality of the child care program itself (Ghazvini & Readdick, 1994).

Parents need to assess their infants' responses and well-being on an ongoing basis. Are positive and nurturing relationships developing among all who share in the care and nurturing of the infant? Does the infant need the routine at home to be more like that of the infant care program, or vice versa? Is the infant overtired or overstimulated from the day's experiences? What is the parent doing to ensure consistency, predictability, and continuity in the infant's life at home? Are the infant's health and safety paramount to all caregivers? Is the infant exhibiting a basic sense of trust, secure attachments, healthy emotional development, and enjoyment of parents and other caregivers? Qualities to assess in seeking appropriate infant care are listed in Figure 6.4. Parents should make informed choices for themselves and their infants, choosing according to the infant's unique developmental needs and the caregiver's ability to meet those needs adequately and appropriately.

## Overall Health, Safety, and Freedom from Stress

Certainly, we can assume that healthy infants are better equipped to deal emotionally and socially with their environments than less healthy infants are. Obstetric and pediatric supervision during prenatal development and infancy provides preventive and corrective measures to facilitate healthy development. Proper nutrition and socially and emotionally satisfying interactions are essential to this health.

Infants who experience chronic illnesses, birth defects, injury, violence, emotionally unstable caregivers, or inconsistent or contradictory child-rearing practices are most likely to develop negative emotionality and psychosocial problems later. Manifestation of these problems in infants depends on factors

**FIGURE 6.4**
Characteristics of
High-Quality
Child Care

1. Trained, knowledgeable, nurturing, and committed caregivers
2. Safe, sanitary, healthy environment for infants and children
3. Low adult-child ratios, with emphasis on providing primary caregivers to individual infants over extended periods of time
4. Cognitively and linguistically enriching, socially stimulating, emotionally supportive environment and caregivers
5. Sensitive, appropriate, antibias interactions and curriculums for all children
6. Sensitivity to parental needs, goals, and concerns
7. Exceeds local and/or state licensing standards
8. Accredited through the National Association for the Education of Young Children

such as age, temperament, past experiences, and bonding and attachment success. Factors relating to the intensity and duration of the problems the infant encounters, including the temperaments and coping abilities of various family members and the willingness and/or ability of the family to seek and benefit from professional help, also influence developmental outcomes.

Infants tend to exhibit signs of stress through physiological functions, such as changes in sleeping and waking patterns, feeding disturbances, heightened emotionality, frantic crying, depressive behaviors, withdrawing, and avoidant behaviors. When these behaviors are evident, parents and professionals might examine the family or child caregiving situation to determine causes and look for solutions. Again, professional counseling may be needed to help the family cope with their difficulties and respond appropriately to the infant.

## Role of the Early Childhood Professional

### Promoting Psychosocial Development in Infants

1. Provide warm, loving, supportive, predictable, consistent, and continuous care.
2. Respond readily to the infant's cues for food, comfort, rest, play, and social interaction.
3. Recognize that crying is the infant's way of communicating their needs.
4. Be aware of sensitive periods relating to attachment behaviors, separation and stranger anxiety, and respond in supportive/empathic ways.
5. Be aware of windows of opportunity and the need for certain essential experiences to promote optimal brain growth and neurological development.
6. Provide stimulating and satisfying social and emotional interactions.
7. Respond readily to the infant's playful overtures.
8. Recognize and accept the infant's unique temperament and ways of interacting with others.
9. Recognize and respond in accepting and supporting ways to the infant's various emotional displays.

## Key Terms

attachment                    separation anxiety        social referencing
fixation                      social cognition          stranger anxiety
reciprocal determinism        socialization

## Review Strategies and Activities

1. Review the key terms independently or with a classmate.

2. Discuss with classmates the differences in the early lives of Angela and Jeremy. In terms of psychosocial development, what kinds of experiences are these infants having? What are the characteristics of the environmental contexts in which each child is developing? What suggestions can you make to enhance the psychosocial development of each child?

3. Review the qualities of a good infant care center. Visit an NAEYC-accredited or other high-quality child care center in which infants are enrolled.

   a. What are the outstanding features of this center?

   b. Would you feel comfortable enrolling your infant in this center?

   c. Observe the interactions between adults and infants: What aspects of psychosocial development do these interactions support (trust, attachment, self-awareness, communication, playfulness, etc.)?

   d. Observe infant's reactions to other infants. What behaviors do they exhibit?

   e. How did the infants respond to you as a stranger? What was the response? How old were the infants whose responses you observed?

   f. How are parents' needs and concerns integrated into the program?

   g. How do the early childhood professionals nurture the psychosocial development of developmentally challenged infants?

4. Interview a working parent to find out how she or he juggles work and parenting. Does this person feel generally positive about his or her lifestyle? What has this person found to be most challenging? Most rewarding?

5. How might parents and/or primary caregivers ensure that infants develop a healthy sense of basic trust? Develop a list of dos and don'ts.

## Further Readings

Bassett, M. M. (1995). *Infant and child care skills.* Albany, NY: Delmar.

Bowe, F. G. (1995). *Birth to five: Early childhood special education.* Albany, NY: Delmar.

Brazelton, T. B. (1994). *Touchpoints: Your child's emotional and behavioral development.* Reading, MA: Addison-Wesley.

Godwin, A., & Schrag, L. Co-Chairs, San Fernando Valley Child Care Consortium (1996). *Setting up for infant/toddler care: Guidelines for centers and family child care homes* (Rev. ed.). Washington, DC: National Association for the Education of Young Children.

Honig, A. S. (1996). *Behavior guidance for infants and toddlers from birth to three years.* Little Rock, AR: Southern Early Childhood Association.

McDonough, H. (1995). *Making home-based child care work for you.* Little Rock, AR: Southern Early Childhood Association.

O'Brien, M. (1997). *Inclusive child care for infants and toddlers: Meeting individual and special needs.* Baltimore, MD: Paul H. Brookes.

Shore, R. (1997). *Rethinking the brain: New insights into early development.* New York: Families and Work Institute.

## OTHER RESOURCES

Association for Childhood Education, International. *Focus on infancy* (A Newsletter for members of the ACEI Professional Division for Infancy. Contact: ACEI, 11501 Georgia Ave., Ste. 315, Wheaton, MD 20902

Video: Magda Gerber (n.d.) *Seeing infants with new eyes.* (26 minutes). Washington, DC: National Association for the Education of Young Children.

Harmes, T., Cryer, D., & Clifford, R.M. (1990). *Infant/toddler environment rating scale.* Washington DC: National Association for the Education of Young Children.

The *zero to three bulletin* (bimonthly)

734 15 Street, N.W., Suite 1000

Washington, DC 20005-1013

Hawley, T. (1998). *Ready to succeed: The lasting effects of early relationships.*

Hawley, T. (1998). *Starting smart: How early experiences affect brain development.*

(Brochures published by Zero to Three, see address above)

CHAPTER SEVEN

# 7

*We are born with the ability to discover the secrets of the universe and of our own minds, and with the drive to explore and experiment until we do. Science isn't just the specialized province of a chilly elite; instead, it's continuous with the kind of learning every one of us does when we're very small.*

ALISON GOPNIK, ANDREW, N. MELTZOFF, AND PATRICIA K. KUHL (1999)

# Cognitive, Language, and Literacy Development of the Infant

*After studying this chapter, you will demonstrate comprehension by:*

▶ Recognizing theoretic perspectives on cognitive, language, literacy development.

▶ Describing cognitive development during the infant's first year.

▶ Describing language development during the infant's first year.

▶ Describing earliest literacy behaviors.

▶ Relating cognitive, language, and literacy development to other developmental areas.

▶ Identifying major factors influencing cognitive, language, and literacy development during infancy.

▶ Suggesting strategies for promoting and enhancing cognitive, language, and literacy development in infancy.

## COGNITIVE DEVELOPMENT IN INFANCY

**Cognitive development** is the aspect of development that deals with thinking, problem solving, intelligence, and language. Infants come into the world with a remarkable capacity to process all kinds of information, from the look and scent of their birth mother and the sound of her voice to sensations of warmth and security or of pain and overstimulation. Over the first few months, the infant will demonstrate quite a repertoire of emerging capabilities and interaction patterns, becoming engaged and curious, communicative and social, and a motoric and active explorer.

**cognitive development:**
The aspect of development that involves thinking, problem-solving, intelligence, and language

## THEORETIC PERSPECTIVES ON COGNITIVE DEVELOPMENT IN INFANCY

As with all other developmental domains, changes in childhood behaviors and abilities over time can be interpreted by reviewing theories advanced by scholars and practitioners in the various disciplines concerned with human growth and development. Chief among the theories of cognitive development are the cognitive/developmental, information processing, social/interactionist, and ecological systems theories. Many aspects of these theories are supported by information from the neurosciences. Neurobiology is shedding light on the neurological processes that are involved in learning, memory, and the complex activities associated with a child's ability to integrate and make sense of internal and external sensory experiences. Let's take a look at these points of view as we begin an intriguing exploration of the developing intellect.

77

## Piaget's Theory of Cognitive Development

The most familiar theory of cognitive development is that of Jean Piaget (1952). Piaget's studies of cognitive development have dominated the fields of child study, psychology, philosophy, and education since the 1920s. He is perhaps the best-known and most widely quoted of the contemporary cognitive theorists. As we will see later in the chapter, other theorists have challenged or modified Piaget's theory; nevertheless, his theory continues to influence knowledge and practice in early childhood education. Foremost among Piaget's contributions to early childhood education is the recognition that the thinking processes and problem-solving abilities of infants and young children are quite different from those of older children and adults. This difference in thinking processes has implications for how parents and caregivers can respond to and interact with infants and young children to promote optimal cognitive development.

*Four Stages of Cognitive Development.*   Piaget's theory proposes four major stages of cognitive development: the sensorimotor period (birth to age two), the preoperational period (ages two to seven), the concrete operations period (ages seven to eleven), and the formal operations period (age eleven and beyond). Table 7.1 provides an overview of these stages and their implications for care and early education. For purposes of this chapter, only the sensorimotor period of infancy will be described, and as cognitive development is discussed in later chapters, each subsequent stage will be summarized.

According to Piaget, all children proceed through a stage-related sequence of cognitive development, each stage building on the accomplishments of the previous one. Piaget viewed these stages as invariant; that is, one stage always follows another in a predictable sequence. All individuals are said to proceed through the invariant sequence, but they do so at their own rates of development. Differences in rates of entering and exiting the stages are attributed to differences in individual genetic timetables and to cultural and environmental influences.

The sensorimotor period extends from birth to the onset of gestures and language at around age two. During this period, the infant's cognitive development depends on direct sensory experiences and motor actions; hence the term **sensorimotor**. Recall the reflexive activities of the newborn described in Chapter 5. These genetically preprogrammed reflexes provide a basis for later cognitive development. Piaget believed that all mental processes are rooted in and are a continuation of the earliest reflexive and motor activities. As the infant gains control over his or her reflexes, movement (or motor) behaviors become more purposeful. Purposeful motor activities facilitate the infant's explorations and hence the infant's awareness of and interactions with objects and people in the environment.

From birth on, through interactions with the environment, the infant begins to form mental structures, which Piaget termed *schemata*. These schemata help the infant to mentally organize and interpret experiences. Each additional experience brings new schemata or perhaps modifies existing schemata. The infant's knowledge of the environment grows through direct actions on objects and experiences with others. Piaget describes the infant at this stage as egocentric, or able to perceive only from his or her own needs, experience, and perspective, not from the perspective of others.

**sensorimotor:** learning that occurs through the senses and motor activities

**Table 7.1.** Piaget's Stages of Cognitive Development

| Stages/Ages | Characteristics | Implications for Interactions and Education |
|---|---|---|
| **Sensorimotor stage** 0 to 2 years | | |
| 1. Reflexive (0 to 1) | Innate reflex responses | Interact in ways that stimulate the infant's sense of touch, taste, sight, sound, and smell |
| 2. Primary circular reactions (1 to 4 months) | Repeats actions that previously happened by change; reflexes becoming more coordinated | Provide sensory stimulating toys and objects such as rattles, mobiles, baby books, recorded familiar voices or pleasing music |
| 3. Secondary circular reactions (4 to 10 months) | Intentionally repeats behaviors or pleasurable actions; the sense of object permanence emerges | Provide clean, safe objects and toys; play hide and seek with them; continue to talk or sing to the infant when moving out of the child's auditory or visual field; play repetitive games |
| 4. Coordination of secondary schemes (10 to 12 months) | Applies previously learned behaviors and activities to new situations; imitative behaviors emerge | Provide familiar toys, dolls, stuffed animals, blankets, and clothing; encourage imitation, provide encouraging verbal feedback |
| 5. Tertiary circular reactions (12 to 18 months) | Cause-and-effect discoveries; seeks proximity and playful interactions with persons to whom attachments have been formed; repeats novel experiences | Respond positively to interaction overtures; provide toys that stack, nest, roll, open, close, push, pull, and are easily manipulated; talk, label, and pretend with child |
| 6. Symbolic representation | Applies learned skills to new situations; begins to think before acting; experiments with new uses for familiar objects; represents objects or events through imagery | Provide verbal labels for objects and events; encourage and provide props for pretend play; provide social interaction with other children; encourage and provide props and safe equipment for large motor activity |
| 2 to 7 years **Preoperational thought** | Ecogentric, perception-bound thinking; more sophisticated language system, rich imagination; performs simple mental operations but has difficulty explaining them | Provide props and toys for imaginative play and exploration, materials for constructions (e.g., crayons, clay, blocks) and a variety of talk, story, music, and pretend opportunities; encourage choices and decision-making; engage in extended meaningful dialogue; encourage new experiences |
| 7 to 11 years **Concrete operational thinking** | Can solve concrete problems with physical objects; thought is reversible; thinking is based on prior experience; the ability to mentally conserve emerges as does simple logic | Provide opportunity to pursue areas of interest; help to obtain materials and resources for exploring and learning; encourage and show interest in school and other activities and accomplishments; engage in meaningful dialogue; use questions to extend understanding |
| 11 years to adulthood **Formal operational thinking** | Formulates and tests hypotheses, abstract thinking, deductive reasoning, thinking is no longer perception-bound and employs logic | Challenge with hypothetical problems to solve, discuss ethical issues; encourage and support educational and hobby interests and abilities; encourage appropriate and enjoyable social interactions |

### Assimilation, Accommodation, and Equilibration.

**adaptation:**
the process by which one adjusts to changes in the environment

According to Piaget, **adaptation** to environmental demands involves two complementary processes: assimilation and accommodation. As infants attempt to fit new ideas and concepts into existing ones, they must assimilate new schemata. At first, the infant visually gazes and tracks and his hands and arms respond to environmental stimuli through reflex activity. Later, these reflexive movements become more integrated into whole activities such as looking and grasping simultaneously or coordinated eye-hand movements. These more integrated responses and movements facilitate the infant's interactions with the objects and people around them, which in turn increase the number and character of the infant's schemata. Each new experience changes the infant's schemata and leads to new learning. New learning builds on previous actions, events, or experiences.

Accommodation is a process by which a previous schema (experience or concept[s]) is modified to include or adapt to a new experience. For example, the breast-fed infant who is changed from breast-feeding (existing schema) to bottle-feeding (new experience) must alter sucking behaviors to succeed with the new experience, the bottle. This altered sucking behavior is an example of accommodation to a new environmental demand. Each assimilation of an experience is complemented by accommodation to that experience, and this leads to adaptation. Adaptation to an event or experience brings about equilibrium between the individual and her or his environment.

Equilibrium is said to occur when assimilation and accommodation are in balance with each other, that is, when the infant has adapted to the demands of the environment. However, this state is usually short-lived, as the infant is constantly being confronted with new information that requires additional assimilations and accommodations.

### Development During the Sensorimotor Stage.

The sensorimotor period of cognitive development is divided into six substages as listed in Figure 7.1. Development through these substages is both rapid and dramatic. During the first year, the infant proceeds through the first four of these substages.

1. Reflexive Stage (birth to one month). During this period, reflexes that have been dominant since birth are modified as the infant experiences an increasing variety of sensory stimuli and interactions with the environment. Piaget believed that the infant constructs schemata from the numerous sensory experiences of these first weeks. The human face or voice, the positioning in the mother's arms before breast-feeding, and the sounds and rhythms of the household are sources of early schemata.

**primary circular reactions:**
simple, repetitive motor activity

2. **Primary circular reactions** (one to four months). At this time, infant reactions center on bodily responses. For example, the infant can now purposefully bring the thumb to the mouth to suck. Previous thumb sucking occurred as a result of accidental and uncoordinated reflex activity. During this stage, the infant engages in other purposeful motor activity. This period is called primary because of its focus on bodily responses; it is called circular because the infant repeats the activities over and over again. This repetition may be the first indication of infant memory.

**secondary circular reactions:**
simple, repetitive responses centered on objects and events in the environment

3. **Secondary circular reactions** (four to eight months). This period is characterized by the infant's enlarging focus on objects and events in the environ-

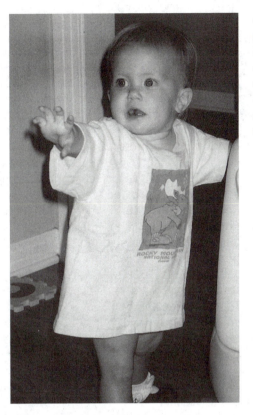

*As infants gain greater mobility through crawling, standing, and walking, their actions are more means/end oriented.*

ment. It is called secondary circular because it involves the infant's growing awareness of objects and events outside his or her own body. Through chance events, the infant learns that he or she can make things happen to external objects. For example, the infant hits the bath water, and a big splash results. This novel experience generates interest and a desire to repeat it; and repeat it the infant does, motivated by both curiosity and pleasure. These behaviors represent early experimentation and become means/ends behaviors. During this substage, infants imitate sounds and actions that they have previously produced and currently hold in their own repertoires. Infants now search for a hidden object, which before this point in development was not pursued if it was not seen. Piaget believed that in the infant's mind, an object not seen did not exist.

4. Coordination of secondary schemata (eight to twelve months). This is the period in which the infant's intentional behaviors are clearly evident. Imitative behaviors signal the infant's growing ability to learn through observing the behavior of others. Play becomes more clearly differentiated from other means/end activities and is enjoyed for its own sake. **Object permanence,** the realization that an object exists even though it cannot be touched or seen, is beginning to emerge.

**object permanence:** the realization that objects and people continue to exist even through they may not be visible or detected through other senses

## Criticisms of the Piagetian Perspective

Some contemporary scholars of cognitive theory (neo-Piagetians, as they are often called) have challenged a number of Piaget's cognitive development assumptions. For instance, Bower (1982) and Wishart and Bower (1985) challenged the notion of object permanence in the infant at six to eight months. Whereas Piaget proposed that an infant will not search for an object hidden behind a screen because the infant believes that the object no longer exists, Bower believes immature space perception may explain the infant's failure to search. He suggests that from the infant's point of view, the screen has replaced the hidden object, and two objects cannot occupy the same space. Bower believes that Piaget underestimated what infants come to know about objects and that their failure to search for or locate a hidden object may represent a lack of spatial knowledge rather than a lack of knowledge of object permanence. Bower suggests that infants as young as five months old will not only anticipate the reappearance of an object that has been moved to a position behind the screen but will attempt to look for it when a different object or no object appears when the screen is removed.

Other researchers have challenged Piaget's notion that infants must do something to or with objects or people in their environment for cognitive development to occur. These scholars suggest that there may be other pathways through which cognition emerges. Studying infants and young children with impaired vision, hearing, and/or motor abilities, they have demonstrated that cognitive development proceeds nonetheless (Bebko, Burke, Craven, & Sarlo, 1992; Furth, 1992a, 1992b, 1992c; Mandler, 1988, 1990, 1992). The belief is that infants, through their perceptual abilities and mental imagery, are able to form concepts with and without direct interaction with objects or people and can do so earlier than Piaget proposed.

While Piaget's theory is characterized by abstract language and ideas that are often hard to translate and to verify through research, his theory remains important to caregivers and educators for several reasons. Piaget's cognitive developmental theory:

- Focuses attention on the sequential aspects of growth and development in the cognitive domain

- Emphasizes the fact that thinking processes in young children are significantly different than thinking processes in older children and adults

- Emphasizes the importance of firsthand, direct, interactional experiences with objects and people

- Provides insight into numerous aspects of cognitive development, such as the development of cause-and-effect relationships; time, space, and number concepts; classification strategies; logic; morality; and language

## Information Processing Theory

The information processing theory (Case, 1985, 1987; Klahr & Wallace, 1976; Shiffrin & Atkinson, 1969; Sternberg, 1985) likens cognitive development to the computer's inputs, throughputs, and outputs. Input refers to the individual's gathering of information from sensory stimuli: vision, hearing, tasting, smelling, tactile sensations, and sensorimotor activity. Input information is then acknowledged, compared to other data already stored in memory, categorized, and stored for future use. This process represents throughput. Subsequent verbal and/or nonverbal responses represent output. Information processing theorists have been variously concerned about how the mind operates during memory, attention, and problem-solving activities. Findings from studies of these cognitive attributes suggest that information processing improves as individuals get older and can develop certain cognitive strategies that assist memory, attention, and problem solving. Nevertheless, information processing theory represents cognitive development as a continuous process in which there are age differences in children's cognitive abilities.

So far, studies have not demonstrated that cognitive strategies for remembering, paying attention and solving problems are evident in infants. In an attempt to explain the adaptive nature of cognitive development, however, Siegler (1991) proposes that "All current theories recognize that people are biologically prepared to perceive the world in certain ways, that many important perceptual capabilities are present at birth, and that others emerge in the first few months of infancy given all but the most abnormal experience" (p. 92). Siegler further asserts that we all perceive the world through our senses, yet learning in infancy inevitably depends on three functions:

Attending: determining what object, event, or action will be mentally processed

Identifying: establishing what a perception is through relating a current perception to perceptions already held in one's memory

Locating: determining where the object of one's perception exists and in what location relative to the observer

## Social Interactionist Theories

Social interactionist theories emphasize the importance of social contexts and role models on learning. Many of these theories have their origins in the behaviorist's point of view in which less importance is given to developmental progressions and more importance to environmental influences. Recall from earlier chapter discussions that the behaviorists (Bijou & Baer, 1961; Skinner, 1938; Watson, 1924) believe that external factors such as reward and punishment have greater impact on individual learning than do innate abilities or biological processes. Social learning theory (Bandura, 1977), which is an outgrowth of the behaviorist philosophy, emphasizes the role of imitation in cognitive development. Many behaviors are learned simply by watching others, and much learning occurs in social situations. It is believed that very young infants can imitate the facial expressions of others (Meltzoff & Moore, 1983) and that infants may have an innate ability to compare information received through different modalities, such as vision, hearing, and their own body movements. They then use this information to coordinate imitative behaviors on the basis of actions observed in others.

## Contextualistic Theory

Still another theoretic perspective that is important in the discussion of cognitive, language, and literacy development in infants is one in which both development and social interaction are viewed as reciprocal influences on one another. Stated quite simply, this theory supposes that the growing and developing child influences and is influenced by his or her environmental context. Contextualistic theories (or ecological systems theory) (Bronfenbrenner, 1977, 1986) are among the most contemporary. They describe cognitive (and language and literacy) development as being integral to the social and cultural context in which an individual grows and develops. Development in all domains (physical/motor, psychosocial, and cognitive, language, and literacy) is viewed as an interactive process between the individual and a variety of social and cultural influences. Cognition continually changes as contexts in which learning occurs change. Cognition, language, and literacy, then, are determined by many factors, including observation and imitation but also opportunities to explore and discover in a variety of situations, both independently and in the company of others, and through coaching and direct instruction. From this perspective, development proceeds to some degree in all domains simultaneously. The degree of influence and rate of development in specific developmental domains depend on the context and nature of the environmental input and the nature and responses of the learner at a given point in time. The following vignettes illustrate this interactive process.

*Jeremy,* lying in his crib, is intently watching a yellow soft-sculpture airplane dangling from the mobile above him. He kicks and squeals with glee, then stops and stares at the object bouncing above his crib. Lying still, he seems to notice that the object stopped swinging; when he kicks some more, the object begins to swing again. The entertainment is quite exhilarating and is repeated several times.

Phyllis, Jeremy's baby-sitter, noticing his playfulness and his interest in the mobile, recognizes that Jeremy has discovered the link between his own bodily movements and the subsequent jiggling of the colorful airplane. She approaches, detaches the airplane from the mobile, and holds it within Jeremy's reach while saying to him, "Do you want to hold the airplane? I think you like this bright toy, Jeremy."

Distracted from his previous activity, Jeremy's kicking subsides. He stares at the soft toy, looks at Phyllis (a bit puzzled), then back again at the toy. His eyes then travel to the mobile above where the airplane had been, then back to Phyllis and the toy in her hand. He reaches for the airplane, grasps it and brings it to his mouth momentarily, then drops it, only to return to the original activity of kicking and watching the mobile. Somehow it isn't the same, and he immediately tires of the effort and begins to fret.

Which of Piaget's sensorimotor substages does Jeremy's behavior exhibit? Approximately how old is Jeremy? If your answer is substage 3, secondary circular reactions, you are correct. If you recalled the approximate age range for this substage, you guessed Jeremy's age to be somewhere between four and eight months. Jeremy is now six months old. His own motor activity that caused the mobile to bounce and swing were entertaining in and of themselves. Jeremy was discovering that his actions could make the airplane wiggle.

However, playful infants attract their caregivers' attention. Phyllis could not resist getting in on the action, but when she did, Jeremy was presented with a choice that was perhaps difficult for him to make: reach for and hold the toy airplane, interact with Phyllis, or continue the pleasurable activity of kicking and watching the mobile move.

While her timing and assumption about what would please Jeremy at that moment missed the mark, Phyllis was supporting Jeremy's cognitive development by noticing what held his attention, naming the object, and bringing it within his reach. Observant adults soon learn to synchronize their interactions with the infant's, recognizing when to enter an activity and when to leave the infant to her or his own explorations.

---

*Angela,* now eight months old, is in her high chair. She still has some difficulty sitting alone and slides under the tray, only to be restrained by the high chair safety strap between her legs. Cracker crumbs are in her hair, on her eyebrows, between her fingers, clinging to her clothing, and sprinkled about on the floor on both sides of her chair. James and Cheryl, seated at the table nearby, have just finished their take-out burgers and are arguing over James's dating activities. It seems that James is seeing some other girls now, and Cheryl is very unhappy about it.

Angela slides under the high chair tray and frets in discomfort. James offhandedly pulls her back into a seated position and continues his emotional discussion with Cheryl. Angela begins to cry intermittently. Cheryl places another cracker on her high chair tray while continuing her emotional conversation with James. Quieted momentarily, Angela bangs the cracker on the tray, holds what is left of it over the floor, then releases her grasp and watches the cracker fall to the floor. Sliding under her tray again, she begins to cry, this time more forcefully. She is pulled back to a seated position by Cheryl, but this does not comfort or quiet her. James, tired of arguing and a bit distracted by the baby's crying, decides to leave.

Frustrated and angry, Cheryl picks up Angela, scolds her about the mess, takes her to the sink to wash her face and hands, then puts her in her playpen, even though Angela is fretful. Unable to respond to Angela's needs—her own are overwhelming at this time—Cheryl turns on the TV, props her feet up on the coffee table, and lapses into sadness.

Unable to elicit her mother's attention, Angela cries awhile longer. Defeated and tired, she picks up her blanket, puts her thumb in her mouth, watches her mother, and listens to the sounds of the television set until she finally falls asleep.

---

Angela's predicament involves psychosocial, physical/motor, and cognitive aspects. At eight months old, what are Angela's cognitive needs? How would you characterize the psychosocial dynamics in this setting between Angela and her caregivers? What does her behavior suggest about her physical/motor development and needs?

Are any apparent constraints to her cognitive development illustrated in this vignette? What alternative activities might be provided for Angela that might engage her attention and contribute to her cognitive development while the adults continue their discussion? What theoretic perspectives can you apply to each of these two scenarios? Let's continue to explore these and other facets of cognitive development.

## The Neurobiology of Cognitive, Language, and Literacy Development

Chapter 5 described the rapid brain growth and neurological development in very young children. This growth and development are so dramatic that during the first ten years, the child's brain will form literally trillions of connections or synapses. This growth includes a process known as myelination in which fatty tissue forms around the nerve cells, facilitating the transportation of impulses along the neurons. Rapid growth and myelination in the brain coincide with the development of the auditory system, rapid language development, and increased processing of visual, spatial, and temporal (or time) information. Simultaneously, these increased connections promote better processing of information, and their presence in the speech center of the brain facilitates the development of symbolization and communication. Gains in short-term memory and small motor skills are also attributed to the rapid myelination occurring during the ages of four and five.

Also, as we have discussed in earlier chapters, the structure and functions of the neurological system are determined by the interplay of experience and an individual's genetically programed blueprint for growth and development. In terms of cognitive, language, and literacy development, of particular importance in earliest brain growth and neurological development is the nature or quality of the child's first interpersonal relationships. As Siegel (1999) so aptly states, "human connections shape the neural connections from which the mind emerges" (p. 2).

These earliest interpersonal relationships shape the neurological structures that establish mental representations of experience in the child's mind. Hence, patterns of relationships and emotional communication, particularly the character of early attachment relationships, influence the brain's biochemistry and subsequent wiring, thus laying down neurological patterns through which the child mentally constructs a view of the world (Siegel, 1999). Further, scholars are now placing significant importance on the role of emotions in the child's attempts to glean meaning from experience. It is believed that the circuits that represent social/emotional experiences are closely linked to those that create representations of meaning. These social/emotional experiences provide a range of stimuli derived from touch and the manner in which the infant is held and handled, voice tone and quality, verbal interactions, facial expressions, eye contact, and the predictability and timing of adult responses to the infant's cues. From these experiences, infants construct their first subjective representations of others. From these experiences, the infant's neurological system establishes patterns of arousal, appraisal, and response—mental activities that are essential to learning. In this regard, it becomes very difficult to separate emotions and cognition because to a great extent from the neurological perspective, they are one and the same (Siegel, 1999). Learning does not occur without emotion.

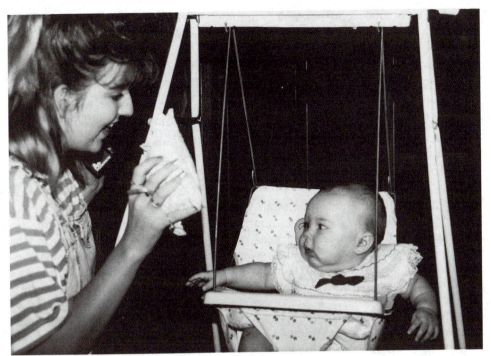

*Playful interactions contribute to early brain growth and neurological development.*

Another important concept associated with early brain growth and neurological development that enlightens our discussion of cognitive development has to do with the importance of timing and types of experiences during infancy and early childhood. It appears that one of the tasks of parenting and teaching is the selection of the "right experiences at the right time" (M. C. Diamond & Hopson, 1998, p. 3). Recall from Chapter 5 (Figure 5.4) that there are windows of opportunity, or critical periods in which the brain is especially vulnerable to certain types of experience (or lack thereof). Much of what is known about critical periods in brain growth have been extrapolated from animal studies. One of the first studies of this nature took place in the 1960s by a group a researchers at the University of California at Berkeley and published under the title "The Effects of Enriched Environments on the Histology of the Rat Cerebral Cortex" (M. C. Diamond, Krech, & Rosenzweig, 1964). This research involved the examination of brain size and density in rats that had been raised in two kinds of cages: an enriched cage that provided toys and a social environment of other rats and a small cage with little to engage the rat's attention and no playmates. The experiments revealed that the rats that were raised in the enriched cage were more competent in navigating mazes than the rats raised in the impoverished cage. Microscopic examination of the rats' dissected brains showed that the enriched rats had a thicker cerebral cortex than the impoverished rats. This experiment demonstrated an actual structural change in the rats' brains based on qualitative differences in their early life experiences (M. C. Diamond et al., 1964). This study opened the door to new ways of thinking about the brain that would emphasize the effects of environment on the biological character of the brain. These researchers over the ensuing decades continued to refine their research techniques and strategies, leading them to project a series of basic principles of brain enrichment such as the following:

- The impact of a stimulating or boring environment affects regions throughout the brains of the experimental rats.
- An enriched environment for pregnant female rats results in newborn pups with thicker cerebral cortex than pups born to impoverished females.
- A boring environment had a more thinning effect on the young and adolescent rat cortex than an exciting environment had on cortex thickening (M. C. Diamond & Hopson, 1998).

So how do these and similar studies influence our thinking about the human brain? Obviously, ethics and common sense prevent the types of environmental controls and anatomical examinations of humans that are possible with laboratory rats. Nevertheless, scientific examination of donated human brain specimens during the early decades of brain research corroborated findings such as those described above; and contemporary technological techniques for examining neurological activity support these early findings (Scheibel, Conrad, Perdue, Tomiyasu, & Wechsler, 1990). In short scholars can now assert that enriched and mentally stimulating environments increase the growth and branching of dendrites and thicken the human cortex. Further, scientists can trace the emergence of various types of development, vision, hearing, motor controls, language, and so on through periods of sensitive and rapid growth delineating certain periods in growth and development when selected experiences have their greater impact. And while brain enrichment is possible throughout the life span, childhood and adolescence appear to be the optimal period for neural development—a time when neural connectivity and pruning and refining are most prolific.

## Sensory and Perceptual Abilities in Infancy

Initially, infants learn through sensations derived from their sensory capabilities: touch, taste, smell, vision, and hearing. Sensations are transmitted to the central nervous system, where interpretation and response take place. Perception is a process by which information gathered through the senses is organized. Recall from Chapter 5 the sensory capabilities of infants. For most infants, vision is reasonably acute, with an ability to visually track an object or a person moving within the infant's visual field. Infants (sometimes within the first few weeks) recognize and respond to the sight, sound, and scent of their mothers. Hearing, taste, and touch are also quite functional. Infants may distinguish their own mothers' voices from other female voices (DeCasper & Fifer, 1980) and can respond differently to infant-directed vocal affect, that is, approving and disapproving tonal qualities and other emotional expressions. It is believed that the infant can make these distinctions in infant-directed speech of several languages (Fernald, 1993). Tactile and kinesthetic sensations complete the sensory repertoire. Thus, the sensory capabilities of infants facilitate reception of environmental stimuli from which perceptions are formed. Perceptions dominate learning in the earliest stages of cognitive, language, and literacy development.

Specific perceptions such as size, shape, weight, distance, and depth, if present at all in early infancy, are imperfect. In efforts to determine specific perceptual abilities of infants, researchers have studied infant responses to facial patterns, geometric patterns, targets that approach and recede from their visual field, looming objects, and depth awareness when placed on an elevated platform. Generally, these perceptions develop over the course of the first year and remain dependent on maturation and integration of all sensory modalities. Experience also contributes to refinement of perceptions. One can imagine, however, the potential for accidents and mishaps during infancy due to faulty perceptions.

While perceptions dominate infant learning in the first months, infant responses to the same stimuli become less noticeable over time as the events occur repeatedly and become familiar to the infant. Vaughn and Litt (1987) refer to the infant's "orienting response," in which the infant is observed to suppress body movements, exhibit alertness, and turn the head toward the stimulus. (Recall Jeremy and the yellow soft-sculpture mobile.) Heartbeat accelerates during this orienting response, and as the stimulus becomes repetitive and familiar, the orienting response habituates; that is, the infant's responses become less and less acute to that particular stimuli. Additional new stimuli elicit new orienting responses.

During the first year, infants become aware of their own bodies and body parts, noticing and gazing at their hands, clasping them together, sucking on fists and fingers, and playing with feet, toes, and genitalia. Emerging coordination of motor skills leads infants to use their bodies and their abilities to explore, experience, and discover. Now there are infinite avenues for learning. The ability to grasp and let go leads to handling, mouthing, and experimenting with a variety of playthings. As the infant manipulates a variety of objects, information about their surroundings is being mentally constructed. The ability to sit, pull to a standing position, cruise around furniture, and return to a seated position provides variety to the infant's sensory experiences and increases the sources of information. The mobility provided by crawling and walking further extends the infant's explorations, experiences, and discoveries.

During the first year, infants also develop self-awareness, the awareness that certain actions on their part result in certain outcomes and responses from their caregivers. Thus, infants learn they can have some control over events and others. Recall from Chapter 6 that positive responses to the infant's cues result in positive feelings about self and feelings of security and trust, qualities that lead to confidence and eagerness to explore the environment and its many possibilities. Success in obtaining caregivers' attentions to needs contributes to the infant's communicative efforts.

# LANGUAGE DEVELOPMENT

One of the most remarkable cognitive achievements of early childhood is the acquisition of language. From beginnings characterized by communication through crying to a variety of interpretable vocal utterances, the infant begins to cognitively construct a very complex communicative system. This system includes focusing attention on another person, gazing and gesturing at sources of sounds, associating certain sounds and voices with particular events and people, developing reciprocity in verbal interactions (as when adult and infant coo back and forth to each other), and learning to use communicative systems to convey needs, feelings, and new learnings. In addition, parents around the world seem to adjust their speech styles when talking to infants, using the simplest words and exaggerating certain vocal sounds and expressions, thus coaxing language along (Fernald & Morikawa, 1993). This altered speech is often referred to as "motherese" or "fatherese."

From the moment of birth, infants seem to be preprogrammed to communicate. They respond readily to the sound of the human voice and have been shown to distinguish the voices of their mothers from other female voices (Mehler, 1985). Infant crying communicates a variety of messages—hunger, discomfort, distress, anger, or boredom—and does so through different intonations and patterns, which become recognizable to the infant's parents and other caregivers. Infants are intensely social, fixing their gaze on the faces of those who talk and sing to them, and are sensitive to the emotional tone of their caregivers. Quite interestingly, in the absence of speech, infants demonstrate remarkable communicative competence.

## Theoretic Perspectives on Language Development

**language acquisition device (LAD):** an innate mental mechanism believed to make language development possible

As with cognitive development, a number of theoretic approaches have attempted to explain language development. A prominent theory proposes an inborn capacity for learning language called the **language acquisition device (LAD)** (Chomsky, 1968, 1980). The LAD is described as a set of innate skills that enable children to infer phoneme patterns, word meanings, and syntax from the language they hear. This skill facilitates the child's own attempts to communicate. The recent scholarship of Steven Pinker (1994) is supportive of this nativistic point of view:

> Language is not a cultural artifact that we learn the way we learn to tell time or how the federal government works. Instead, it is a distinct piece of the biological makeup of our brains. Language is a complex, specialized skill, which develops in the child spontaneously, without conscious effort or formal instruction, is deployed without awareness of its underlying logic, is qualitatively the same in every individual, and is distinct from more general abilities to process information or behave intelligently. (Pinker, 1994, p. 18)

In short, this scholar believes that the development of language is an instinctual process.

The nativist and instinctual perspectives assume a biological basis for human language, one that supposes that language emerges because there are specialized structures in the brain and neurological systems of humans. Studies of language development in children with hearing loss, of children who have suffered brain injury to the left brain hemisphere, and of the immigrant's acquisition of a new language after early childhood have demonstrated that there is a critical period or window of opportunity for language development. For example, when infants who are deaf are raised by parents who communicate through signing, the infants learn sign language in the same manner and with the same ease as hearing infants learn spoken language and come to use this form of communication quite competently as they get older. Deprived of opportunities to learn sign language from infancy onward, deaf children struggle as they get older to gain skill in signing and seldom truly master this form of communication (Pinker, 1994). Because of the plasticity of the language-learning circuitry in the brain, children with left brain hemispheric injury or removal recover language to a greater extent than do adults with comparable injury. By the same token, younger immigrants acquire a new language, including accents and inflections, more completely and accurately than do their teenage or adult relatives. Between birth and age six years appears to be a biological prime time for the acquisition of language.

A behaviorist point of view, in contrast, holds that infants gradually learn languages through imitation of the sounds and speech they hear. When the infant spontaneously, and often accidentally, creates or repeats a sound and the parents respond with joy and encouragement, vocal productions become pleasurable experiences worth repeating (Skinner, 1957). Language is believed to be taught through reinforcement in the form of attention, repetition, and approval.

The social interactionist point of view emphasizes the importance of the infant's interactions with caregivers in which vocal exchanges occur (Bruner, 1975, 1983; Golinkoff, 1983). These researchers recognize the communicative aspects of these early vocal exchanges and the emotional satisfaction that accrues from successful exchanges between caregiver and child. Indeed, language in humans is dependent on having other humans with whom to communicate.

A social interactionist view of language development takes into consideration the interplay of many factors, including the biological underpinnings of language, maturational patterns, cognitive development and the role of imitation, teaching and learning, and the necessity of social interaction. Through an interactive process, these factors play on one another in ways that encourage or impede language development.

## Language Development in the First Year

The development of speech in the first year of life varies from child to child. A few children speak in sentences by the end of the first year. Others use only one-word "sentences" that can be understood only by those who participate consistently in the infant's everyday care. Piaget (1926) thought that cognition influences language. Since he viewed infants and young children as egocentric, Piaget therefore concluded that earliest speech is egocentric. He observed that the speech of infants and young children appears to be addressed to no one in particular. Vygotsky (1934/1962) believed that language influences cognition and that the speech of infants and young children is not egocentric but is communication with the self.

Under normal circumstances, infants follow similar, predictable sequences in the development of language. This seems to be true regardless of geography or culture. As with other areas of development, most children follow a predictable pattern, but not all children proceed through the sequences at the same rate. The sequence for language development during the first year is illustrated in Table 7.2.

As was noted earlier, crying conveys a variety of messages, and caregivers soon learn to interpret the sounds and intensities of the infant's cries and respond appropriately. Around age 4 weeks, infants make small, throaty noises that are perhaps precursors to the vowel sounds that will begin to appear around eight weeks. Infants discover their own voices around twelve weeks and

## TABLE 7.2. Milestones in Language Development

| Age | Phonology | Morphology and Semantics | Syntax | Pragmatics |
|---|---|---|---|---|
| Birth | Crying | | | |
| 1 month | Attends and responds to speaking voice | | | |
| 2 months | Cooing, distinguishes phoneme features | | | |
| 3 months | Vocalizes to social stimulus | | | |
| 4 months | Chuckles | | | Pointing and gestures |
| 6 months | Babbling | | | |
| 9 months | Echolalia | Understands a few words | | Understands gestures; responds to "bye-bye" |
| 12 months | Repeated syllables, jabbers expressively | First word | | Waves "bye-bye" |
| 18 months | | Comprehends simple questions, points to nose, eyes, and hair, vocabulary of 22 words | Two-word utterances, telegraphic speech | Uses words to make wants known |
| 24 months | | Vocabulary of 272 words | Uses pronouns and and prepositions; uses simple sentences and phrases | Conversational turn-taking |

*Source:* From the manual of the Bayley Scales of Infant Development. Copyright 1969 by The Psychological Corporation, a Harcourt Assessment Company. Reproduced by permission. All rights reserved.

enjoy gurgling and cooing, repeating the same vowel sound over and over, with perhaps some variation in tone. The infant is content to play with his or her voice alone or in concert with a parent or caregiver. Laughing aloud also occurs about this time. Infants are thought to view this exchange as a noise-making activity in which infant and others "speak" at the same time (Rosenthal, 1982).

Around six months of age, babbling begins to occur in which the vowel sounds are combined with the consonants m, p, b, k, and g. Babbles such as "bababa" are repeated over and over in succession, producing **echolalia**. It is

**echolalia:**

the infant's repetitive babbling of one sound

believed that regardless of culture or locale, children all over the world produce similar babbles (Olney & Scholnick, 1976). As infants get older, linguists are able, through the use of tape recordings of infant vocalizations, to distinguish subtle differences in the babbles of children in different environments (DeBoysson-Bardies, Sagart, & Durand, 1984). This is possible at around six to seven months, when babbling becomes more varied in intonation, loudness, and rhythm and additional consonants are produced. Infants at this age begin to take turns in their vocalizations with a parent or caregiver (Rosenthal, 1982).

During the latter half of the first year, infants are learning about the sounds of their native language and begin to make distinctions between their native language and other languages (Juscyzk, Cutler, & Redanz, 1993). Around eight to ten months, the infant may vocalize with toys, as though talking to them. Streams of babbles that sound like a conversation occur, yet no meaningful words emerge in this rich array of sounds. The infant may use sounds that approximate words or that are his or her own creation to represent objects or events. These sounds are called **vocables** (Ferguson, 1977). Later in this period, the infant may have learned a few isolated words. These words may or may not have true meaning for the infant and probably are not associated with actual objects or people. Sometimes, the streams of babbles include the interjection of an occasional word, creating a kind of pseudolanguage.

**vocables:**
early sound patterns, used by infants, that approximate words

By the end of the first year, the infant may use one or two words correctly and comprehend simple commands and phrases, such as "no-no" and "bye-bye," and some nonverbal language in the form of gestures, such as "come to Daddy" and "peek-a-boo." Infants respond to their own names and know the names of a few objects, though they may not speak these names. **Holophrases,** in which one word or syllable represents a whole sentence, may emerge (e.g., "baba" means "I want my bottle").

**holophrases:**
the use of one word to convey a phrase or a sentence

Of interest to researchers and parents alike is the emergence of first words. Katherine Nelson refers to the infant's growing awareness of two different worlds: objects and people (Nelson, 1973, 1979; Nelson & Lucariello, 1985). During the latter half of the first year, infants begin to realize that these different entities provide different experiences. Nelson argues that coordination of these two worlds is essential for the development of language. First words, **overgeneralized speech,** represent one or the other category; for instance, "ball" may come to represent all toys, not just the child's ball. "Mama," on the other hand, may come to imply a full message to someone about the infant's need. Nelson places some emphasis on the interactive experiences infants have with adults who are aware of and in tune with emerging language. Parents and caregivers who engage in focused "conversations" with their infants and continually provide names and descriptions of objects and events around them support and enhance language development during this important period.

**overgeneralized speech:**
the use of a single word or label to represent an entire category of objects similar in use or appearance

## LITERACY DEVELOPMENT

Literacy has it origins in a variety of infant experiences and sensations. Listening to and engaging in vocal interactions with others, tuning into the sounds and rhythms of the voices and language surrounding them, observing the facial expressions of their caregivers, and visually fixating on objects of interest begin

*The orgins of literacy occur during the infant and toddler period.*

the journey toward literacy. On the basis of the belief that the origins of literacy occur in infancy, researchers in language and literacy development suggest that infants benefit from and enjoy sharing chants, rhymes, songs, playful games of peek-a-boo and pat-a-cake, and baby books with their parents and caregivers. Hearing softly spoken language with the rich intonations that accompany stories and songs is an enriching and enjoyable auditory and cognitive experience for infants that leads to heightened interest in both the spoken word and books.

Further, infants can be provided appropriate baby books to view and handle, beginning with heavy cardboard baby books using very simple, single familiar item pictures. The board book (as this type of book is called) can be stood in the corner of the crib or within the infant's view to provide an engaging visual experience. As the infant gains motor controls and can reach and bring items to his or her mouth, a different type of book is preferable, one that is made of fabric or another soft washable material. Gradually, as infants become less physical and more visual in their relationships with books, their interest in the pictures and stories of books increases. Using baby books to engage older infants in very simple point-and-name activities ("This is a ball," "See the kitten?") engages the infant, enhances interest and curiosity, and begins a process whereby infants begin to form visual symbolic representations in their minds.

Linda Lamme (1980) describes five categories of literature for infants: musical literature; point-and-say books; touch-and-smell books; cardboard, cloth, and plastic books; and early stories. Establishing routines in the infant's day that include shared time with such literature enhances parent-child communication, facilitates language development, and lays the foundation for later reading abilities.

# FACTORS INFLUENCING COGNITION, LANGUAGE, AND LITERACY DEVELOPMENT

Think again about Jeremy and Angela. From the descriptions of their lives so far, several factors influencing development in all areas are beginning to evident. Compare the lives of Jeremy and Angela in terms of the factors that influence cognition, language, and literacy.

1. Full-term infants get off to a healthier, less vulnerable start in life. Optimal health from the beginning facilitates all development—physical and motor, psychosocial, cognitive, language, and literacy.

2. The integrity of the sensory mechanisms, particularly hearing and vision, influence the extent to which these modalities can support and enhance learning and the extent to which compensating mechanisms come into play.

3. Proper nutrition is essential to good health and supports optimal brain and neurological development. There is evidence that appropriate and adequate nutrition during the earliest months is critical for brain growth and neurological development; in severe cases of malnutrition during the first six months, the deleterious effects can be irreversible.

4. Environments that support the infant's cognitive, language, and literacy development with engaging social interaction, enriching sensory stimuli, opportunities for motor exploration, appropriate playthings and baby books, promote optimal development.

5. Interactions with others who are responsive, supportive, and stimulating enhance not only the psychosocial development of the infant but cognition, language, and literacy development as well.

Adults may facilitate and enhance infant cognition, language development, and emerging literacy in a number of ways. Development cannot be hurried, and any efforts should first take cues from the behaviors of the infant. Bombarding the infant with too many stimuli, inappropriate toys, visually and auditorially overstimulating environments, and expectations that exceed their current capabilities is confusing to an infant and can impede optimal psychosocial and cognitive development. In confusing and overstimulating circumstances, infants become irritable and stressed, sometimes become depressed, and may exhibit problems with eating, sleeping, attending, and playing. An appreciation of the infant's own developmental timetable guides parents and caregivers.

## Role of the Early Childhood Professional

### Promoting Cognitive, Language, and Literacy Development in Infants

1. Engage readily in social interaction with the infant, responding to the infant's cues for social and emotional support.

2. Provide an enriched social environment that includes opportunities for the infant to watch, interact with, and feel and be a part of the family or child care group.

3. Provide a safe, supportive, and nurturing environment that encourages exploration beyond the crib or playpen.

4. Provide a sensory-rich environment, including vocal and verbal interactions with the infant, soft singing, shared baby books, story reading, bright and cheerful surroundings, visual access to windows, simple, uncluttered pictures on the wall, and other visual interests.

5. Provide appropriate auditory stimuli, including talk and laughter, singing, chanting, reading or playing taped music, and other sources of interesting sounds, such as wind chimes.

6. Vary tactile stimuli with appropriate stuffed toys and soft sculptured items made from a variety of textures.

7. Periodically alter the child's scenery: Move the crib to another side of the room, move the high chair to another side of the table, occasionally change the visuals on the wall around the crib or play areas.

8. Provide safe, simple, engaging, age-appropriate toys and crib items, and replace them when the infant's interest in them wanes.

9. Explore the surroundings with the infant, carrying him or her about, gazing into the mirror, pointing to a photograph on the wall, looking through the window, finding the lowest kitchen drawer and examining its safe and intriguing contents, and so on.

10. Take older infants on brief outings with you. Talk about where you are going, what you are doing, what you are seeing. Name objects, places, and people as you go.

11. Place an older infant's toys on low, open shelves for easy access and cleanup.

12. Respond with focused interest and enthusiasm to the infant's attempts to initiate playfulness and interaction.

## KEY TERMS

adaptation
cognitive
   development
echolalia
holophrases

language acquisition
   device (LAD)
object permanence
overgeneralized speech
primary circular reactions

secondary circular
   reactions
sensorimotor
vocables

# REVIEW STRATEGIES AND ACTIVITIES

1. Review the key terms individually or with a classmate.

2. This and other chapters have introduced a variety of theories associated with growth and development in young children. Angela and Jeremy have provided examples of development during the first year. Reread the stories of Angela and Jeremy appearing in previous chapters. On the basis of what you have learned so far about child development, make a list of your observations about Angela's and Jeremy's development and reflect on their potential. Discuss and compare your lists and reflections with those of your classmates.

3. Describe a child care program that offers optimal opportunities for cognitive, language, and literacy development. What types of interactions take place in these settings? How is cognitive, language, and literacy development supported through the activities and materials provided for infants?

4. Tape-record the vocalizations of an infant between the ages of five months and twelve months. With pencil in hand, listen to the various sounds the infant makes and record the vowels and consonants you think you hear. Which ones occur most often? Describe the tonal quality of the vocalizations. How long did each last? What events stimulated and/or prolonged the vocalizations? Compare your findings with the descriptions in this chapter.

# FURTHER READINGS

Acredolo, L., & Goodwyn, S. (1996). *Baby signs: How to talk with your baby before your baby can talk*. Chicago, IL: Contemporary Books.

Ard, L., & Pitts, M. (Eds.). (1995). *Room to grow: How to create quality early childhood environments*. Austin, TX: Texas Association for the Education of Young Children.

Bredekamp, S., & Copple, C. (Eds.). (1997). *Developmentally appropriate practices in early childhood programs* (Rev. ed.). Washington, DC: National Association for the Education of Young Children.

Bronson, M. B. (1995). *The right stuff for children birth to 8: Selecting play materials to support development*. Washington, DC: National Association for the Education of Young Children.

Cochenour, D. (1994). *Learning all day: Curriculum for infants and toddlers*. Little Rock, AR: Southern Early Childhood Association.

Diamond, M. C., & Hopson, J. (1998). *Magic trees of the mind: How to nurture your child's intelligence, creativity, and healthy emotions from birth through adolescence*. New York: Plume Books.

Gopnik, A., Meltzoff, A., & Kuhl, P. (1999). *The scientist in the crib*. New York: William Morrow & Company.

Greenspan, S. I. (1997). *The growth of the mind and the endangered origins of intelligence*. Reading, MA: Addison-Wesley.

Hodge, S., with E. Morsund (Illustrator). (1995). *Caring for infants and toddlers with special needs*. Little Rock, AR: Southern Early Childhood Association.

Neuman, S. B., Copple, C., & Bredekamp, S. (2000). *Learning to read and write: Developmentally appropriate practices for young children*. Washington, DC: National Association for the Education of Young Children.

Ramey, C. T., & Ramey, S. L. (1999). *Right from birth: Building your child's foundation for life (birth to 18 months)*. New York: Goddard Press.

Schickedanz, J. A. (1999). *Much more than the ABCs: The early stages of reading and writing*. Washington, DC: National Association for the Education of Young Children.

Vaughn, E., with E. Morsund (Illustrator) (1993). *Books for babies: Using books with infants and toddlers*. Little Rock, AR: Southern Early Childhood Association.

# References

Adair, R., Baucher, H., Philipp, B., Levenson, S., & Zuckerman, B. (1991). Night waking during infancy: Role of parental presence at bedtime. *Pediatrics, 87*(4), 500–504.

Adams, G. C., & Poersch, N. O. (1997). *Key facts about child care and early education: A briefing book.* Washington, DC: Children's Defense Fund.

Adams, R. J., Mauer, D., & Davis, M. (1986). Newborns' discrimination of chromatic from achromatic stimuli. *Journal of Experimental Child Psychology, 41,* 267–281.

Adamson, L. B., & Bakeman, R. (1985). Affect and attention: Infants observed with mothers and peers. *Child Development, 56,* 582–593.

Ainsworth, M. D. S. (1962). The effects of maternal deprivation: A review of findings and controversy in the context of research strategy. In World Health Organization, *Deprivation of maternal care: A reassessment of its effects* (Public Health Paper No. 14, pp. 97–165). Geneva: Author.

Ainsworth, M. D. S. (1967). *Infancy in Uganda: Infant care and the growth of love.* Baltimore: The John Hopkins Press.

Ainsworth, M. D. S. (1973). The development of infant-mother attachment. In B. M. Caldwell & H. N. Riccluti (Eds.), *Review of child development research* (Vol. 3, pp. 1–94). Chicago: University of Chicago Press.

Ainsworth, M. D. S., Bell, S. M., & Stayton, D. J. (1974). Infant-mother attachment and social development: Socialization as a product of reciprocal responsiveness to signals. In M. P. M. Richards (Ed.), *The integration of the child into a social world* (pp. 99–135). London: Cambridge University Press.

Ainsworth, M. D. S., Blehar, M. C., Waters, E., & Wall, S. (1978). *Patterns of attachment: A psychological study of strange situations.* Hillsdale, NJ: Erlbaum.

Ainsworth, M. D. S., & Wittig, B. A. (1969). Attachment and the exploratory behavior of one-year-olds in a strange situation. In B. M. Foss (Ed.), *Determinants of infant behavior* (Vol. 4, pp. 113–136). London: Methuen.

American Academy of Family Physicians. (1996). *Recommended core educational guidelines for family practice residents.* Kansas City, MO: Author.

American Academy of Pediatrics. (1993). *Pediatric nutrition handbook.* Elk Grove Village, IL: Author.

American Academy of Pediatrics. (1998). *A woman's guide to breastfeeding.* Elk Grove Village, IL: Author.

American Academy of Pediatrics and American College of Obstetricians and Gynecologists. (1992). Postpartum and follow-up care. In *Guidelines for perinatal care.* Elk Grove Village, IL: American Academy of Pediatrics.

American Academy of Pediatrics Committee on Child Abuse and Neglect. (1994). Distinguishing sudden infant death syndrome from child abuse and fatalities. *Pediatrics, 94*(1), 124–126.

American Academy of Pediatrics Work Group on Breastfeeding. (1997). Breastfeeding and the use of human milk. *Pediatrics, 100*(6), 1035–1039.

American Public Health Association and American Academy of Pediatrics. (1992). *Caring for our children: National health and safety performance standards: Guidelines for out-of-home child care.* Washington, DC, and Elk Grove Village, IL: Author.

Anastasi, A. (1958). Heredity, environment, and the question: How? *Psychological Review, 65*(4), 197–208.

Anselmo, S. (1987). *Early childhood development: Prenatal through age eight.* Columbus, OH: Merrill.

Arnold, L. D. W., & Tully, M. R. (Eds.) (1996). *Guidelines for the establishment and operation of a donor human milk bank.* West Hartford, CT: Human Milk Banking Association of North America.

Bandura, A. (1977). *Social learning theory.* Englewood Cliffs, NJ: Prentice-Hall.

Bandura, A. (1986). *Social foundation of thoughts and actions: A social cognitive theory.* Englewood Cliffs, NJ: Prentice Hall.

Barbero, G. J., & Shaheen, E. (1967). Environmental failure to thrive: A clinical view. *Journal of Pediatrics, 71,* 639–644.

Bebko, J. M., Burke, L., Craven, J., & Sarlo, N. (1992). The importance of motor activity in sensorimotor development: A perspective from children with physical handicaps. *Human Development, 35*(4), 226–240.

Bell, S. M., & Ainsworth, M. D. S. (1972). Infant crying and maternal responsiveness. *Child Development, 43,* 1171–1190.

Belsky, J. (1988). The effects of infant day care reconsidered. *Early Childhood Research Quarterly, 3,* 235–272.

Belsky, J., & Rovine, M. (1988). Non-maternal care in the first year of life and the security of infant-parent attachment. *Child Development, 59*(1), 157–167.

Bench, J. (1978). The auditory response. In V. Stave (Ed.), *Perinatal physiology.* New York: Plenum Press.

Berg, W. K., Adkinson, C. D., & Strock, B. D. (1973). Duration and frequency of periods of alertness in neonates. *Developmental Psychology, 9,* 434.

Bijou, S., & Baer, D. (1961). *Child development: Vol. 1. A systematic and empirical theory.* Englewood Cliffs, NJ: Prentice-Hall.

Blass, E. M., & Shah, A. (1995). Pain-reducing properties of sucrose in human newborns. *Chemical Senses, 20*(1), 29–35.

Bornstein, M. H. (1984). A descriptive taxonomy of psychological categories used by infants. In C. Sophian (Ed.), *Origins of cognitive skills. The eighteenth annual Carnegie Symposium on Cognition* (pp. 313–338). Hillsdale, NJ: Erlbaum.

Bornstein, M. H. (1985). Human infant color vision and color perception. *Infant Behavior and Development, 8,* 109–113.

Bornstein, M. H. (1988). Perceptual development across the life cycle. In M. H. Bornstein, & M. E. Lamp (Eds.), *Developmental psychology: An advanced textbook* (2nd ed., pp. 151–204). Hillsdale, NJ: Erlbaum.

Bornstein, M. H., & Lamb, M. E. (1992). *Development in infancy: An introduction* (3rd ed.). New York: McGraw-Hill.

Bower, T. G. R. (1982). *Development in infancy* (2nd ed.). New York: Freeman.

Bowlby, J. (1969/1982). *Attachment and loss: Vol. 1. Attachment* (2nd ed.). New York: Basic Books.

Bowlby, J. (1973). *Attachment and loss: Vol. 2. Separation: Anxiety and anger.* New York: Basic Books.

Bowlby, J. (1980). *Attachment and loss: Vol. 3. Loss: Sadness and depression.* New York: Basic Books.

Brazelton, T. B. (1992). *Touchpoints: The essential reference: Your child's emotional and behavioral development.* Reading, MA: Addison-Wesley Publishing Company.

Brecht, M. C. (1989). The tragedy of infant mortality. *Nursing Outlook, 37*(18).

Bredekamp, S. (Ed.). (1991). Accreditation criteria and procedures of the National Academy of Early Childhood Programs. Washington, DC: National Association for the Education of Young People.

Bretherton, I., & Walters, E. (Eds.). (1985). Growing points in attachment theory and research. *Monographs of the Society for Research in Child Development, 50*(1–2, Serial No. 209).

Bronfenbrenner, U. (1977). Toward an experimental ecology of human development. *American Psychologist, 32,* 513–531.

Bronfenbrenner, U. (1979). *The ecology of human development.* Cambridge, MA: Harvard University Press.

Bronfenbrenner, U. (1986). Ecology of the family as a context for human development: Research perspectives. *Developmental Psychology, 22,* 723–742.

Bruner, J. (1975). The ontogenesis of speech acts. *Journal of Child Language, 3,* 1–19.

Bruner, J. (1983). The acquisition of pragmatic commitments. In R. M. Golinkoff (Ed.), *The transition from prelinguistic to linguistic communication* (pp. 27–42). Hillsdale, NJ: Erlbaum.

Burchinal, M. R., Bryant, D. M., Lee, M. V., & Ramey, C. T. (1992). Early day care, infant-mother attachment, and maternal responsiveness in the infant's first year. *Early Childhood Research Quarterly, 7,* 383–396.

Buss, A. H., & Plomin, R. (1984). *Temperament: Early developing personality traits.* Hillsdale, NJ: Erlbaum.

Campos, J. J., Barrett, K. C., Lamb, M. L., Goldsmith, H. H., & Stenberg, C. (1983). Socioemotional development. In M. M. Haith & J. J. Campos (Eds.), *Infancy and developmental psychobiology* (pp. 783–915). New York: Wiley.

Campos, J. J., & Stenberg, C. R. (1981). Perception appraisal and emotion: The onset of social referencing. In M. E. Lamb & L. R. Sherrod (Eds.), *Infant social cognition: Empirical and theoretical considerations* (pp. 273–314). Hillsdale, NJ: Erlbaum.

Caron, A. J., Caron, R. F., & MacLean, D. (1988). Infant discrimination of naturalistic emotional expressions: The role of face and voice. *Child Development, 59,* 604–616.

Case, R. (1985). *Intellectual development: A systematic reinterpretation.* New York: Freeman.

Case, R. (1987). Neo-Piagetian theory: Retrospect and prospect. In A. Demetriou (Ed.), *The neo-Piagetian theories of cognitive development: Toward an integration.* Amsterdam: North Holland.

Cassidy, J., & Berlin, L. J. (1994). The insecure/ambivalent patterns of attachments: Theory & research. *Child Development, 65*(4), 971–991.

Centers for Disease Control. (1992). Retrospective assessment of vaccination coverage among school-aged children—selected United States cities, 1991. *MMWR, 41,* 103–107.

Chance, N. (1984). Growing up in a Chinese village. *Natural History, 93,* 78–81.

Chess, S. (1967). Temperament in the normal infant. In B. Straub & J. Hellmuth (Eds.), *Exceptional infant: Vol. 1. The normal infant* (pp. 143–162). Seattle, WA: Special Child Publications.

Chess, S., & Thomas, A. (1987). *Origins and evolution of behavior disorders from infancy to early adult life.* Cambridge, MA: Harvard University Press.

Children's Defense Fund. (1999). *The state of America's children Yearbook, 1999.* Washington, DC: Author.

Chomsky, N. (1968). *Language and mind.* San Diego, CA: Harcourt Brace Jovanovich.

Chomsky, N. (1980). *Rules and representations.* New York: Columbia University Press.

Christian, J. L., & Gregor, J. L. (1988). *Nutrition for living* (2nd ed.). Menlo Park, CA: Benjamin/Cummings.

Chugani, H. T. (1997). Neuroimaging of developmental non-linearity and developmental pathologies. In R. W. Thatcher, G. R. Lyon, J. Rumsey, & N. Krasnegor (Eds.), *Developmental neuroimaging: Mapping the development of brain and behavior.* San Diego: Academic Press.

Clyman, R. B., Emde, R. N., Kempe, J. E., & Harmon, R. J. (1986). Social referencing and social looking among 12-month-old infants. In T. B. Brazelton & M. W. Yogman (Eds.), *Affective development in infancy* (pp. 75–94). Norwood, NJ: Ablex.

Comer, J. P., & Poussant, A. F. (1992). *Raising black children.* New York: Penguin Books.

Cornell, E. H., & McDonnell, P. M. (1986). Infants' acuity at twenty feet. *Investigative Ophthalmology and Visual Science, 27,* 1417–1420.

Davis, D. W., & Bell, P. A. (1991). Infant feeding practices and occlusal outcomes: A longitudinal study. *Journal of the Canadian Dental Association, 57*(7), 593–594.

DeBoysson-Bardies, B., Sagart, L., & Durand, C. (1984). Discernible differences in the babbling of infants according to target language. *Journal of Child Language, 11,* 1–16.

DeCasper, A. J., & Fifer, W. P. (1980). Of human bonding: Newborns prefer their mother's voices. *Science, 208,* 1174–1176.

Delcomyn, F. (1998). *Foundations of neurobiology.* New York: W. H. Freeman.

Diamond, M. C., & Hopson, J. (1998). *Magic trees of the mind.* New York: Plume Books.

Diamond, M. C., Krech, D., & Rosenzweig, M. R. (1964). The effects of an enriched environment on the histology of the rat cerebral cortex. *Journal of Comparative Neurology, 123,* 111–120.

Dienstbier, R. A. (January, 1989). Arousal and physiological toughness: Implications for mental and physical health. *Psychological Review, 96*(1), 84–100.

Dobbing, J. (1984). Infant nutrition and later achievement. *Nutrition Reviews, 42,* 1–7.

Easterbrooks, M. A., & Goldberg, W. A. (1990). Toddler-parent attachment: Relation to children's sociopersonality functioning during kindergarten. In M. T. Greenberg, D. Cicchetti, & E. M. Cummings (Eds.), *Attachment in the preschool years: Theory, research and intervention* (pp. 221–224). Chicago: University of Chicago Press.

Eaton, W. O., Chipperfield, J. G., & Singbell, C. E. (1989). Birth order and activity level in children. *Developmental Psychology, 25,* 668–672.

Emde, R. N., & Harmon, R. J. (1972). Endogenous and exogenous smiling systems in early infancy. *Journal of the American Academy of Child Psychiatry, 11,* 177–200.

Fagot, B. I., & Kavanagh, K. (1990). The prediction of antisocial behaviors from avoidant attachment classifications. *Child Development, 61*(3), 863–873.

Fantz, R. L. (1961). The origin of form perception. *Scientific American, 204,* 66–72.

Federal Interagency Forum on Child and Family Statistics. (1999). *America's children: Key national indicators of well-being.* Federal Interagency Forum on Child and Family Statistics, Washington, DC: U.S. Government Printing Office.

Fein, G., Gariboldi, A., & Boni, R. (1993). The adjustment of infants and toddlers to group care: The first 6 months. *Early Childhood Research Quarterly, 8*(1), 1–14.

Ferguson, C. A. (1977). Learning to pronounce: The earliest stages of phonological development in the child. In F. D. Minifie & L. L. Lloyd (Eds.), *Communicative and cognitive abilities: Early behavioral assessment* (pp. 141–155). Baltimore: University Park Press.

Fernald, A. (1993). Approval and disapproval: Infant responsiveness to vocal affect in familiar and unfamiliar languages. *Child Development, 64*(3), 657–674.

Fernald A., & Morikawa, H. (1993). Common themes and cultural variations in Japanese and American mothers' speech to infants. *Child Development, 64*(3), 637–656.

Field, T. M. (1979). Differential behavioral & cardiac responses of 3-month-old infants to a mirror and a peer. *Infant Behavior and Development, 2,* 179–184.

Field, T. M. (1982). Individual differences in the expressivity of neonates and young infants. In R. Feldman (Ed.), *Development of nonverbal behavior in children* (pp. 279–298). New York: Springer-Verlag.

Field, T. M., Schanberg, S. M., Scafidi, F., Bauer, C. R., Vegalahr, N., Garcia, R., Nystrom, J., & Kuhn, C. M. (1986). Effects of tactile/kinesthetic stimulation on preterm neonates. *Pediatrics, 77,* 654–658.

Fike, R. D. (1993). Personal relationship-building between fathers and infants. Association for Childhood Education International Theme Issue: Focus on Infancy. *Childhood Education, 5*(4), 1–2.

Fogel, A. (1979). Peer vs. mother directed behavior in 1- to 3-month-old infants. *Infant Behavior and Development, 2,* 215–226.

Freud, S. (1933). *New introductory lectures on psychoanalysis.* New York: Norton.

Fuller, B., Eggers-Pierola, C., Holloway, S.D. Liang, X., & Rambaud, M. (1995). Rich culture, poor markets: Why do Latino parents choose to forego preschooling? In B. Fuller, R. Elmore, & G. Orfield (Eds.). *School choice: The cultural logic of families, the political rationality of institutions.* New York: Teachers College Press.

Furth, H. G. (1992a). The developmental origin of human societies. In H. Beilin and P. B. Pufall (Eds.), *Piaget's theory: Prospects and possibilities.* Hillsdale, NJ: Erlbaum.

Furth, H. G. (1992b). Life's essential—The story of mind over body: A review of "I raise my eyes to say yes": A memoir by Ruth Sienkiewicz-Mercer & S. B. Kaplan. *Human Development, 35*(2), 254–261.

Furth, H. G. (1992c). Commentary on Bebko, Burke, Craven & Sarlo (1992): The importance of sensorimotor development: A perspective from children with physical handicaps. *Human Development, 36*(4), 226–240.

Galler, J. R., Ramsey, F., & Solimano, G. (1984). The influence of early malnutrition on subsequent development: 3. Learning disabilities as a sequel to malnutrition. *Pediatric Research, 18,* 309.

Galler, J. R., Ramsey, F., & Solimano, G. (1985). A follow-up study of the effects of early malnutrition on subsequent development: 2. Fine motor skills in adolescence. *Pediatric Research, 19,* 524.

Garcia-Coll, C. T. (1990). Developmental outcomes of minority infants: A process-oriented look into our beginnings. *Child Development, 61*(2), 270–289.

Garrett, P., Ferron, J., Ng'Andu, N., Bryant, D., & Harbin, G. (1994). A structural model for the developmental status of young children. *Journal of Marriage and the Family, 56*(1), 147–163.

Gazzaniga, M. (1988). *Mind matters: How mind and brain interact to create our conscious lives.* Boston: Houghton Mifflin, in association with MIT Press.

Gelles, R. J., & Edfeldt, A. W. (1990). Violence toward children in the United States and Sweden. In M. A. Jensen & Z. W. Chevalier (Eds.), *Issues and advocacy in early education* (pp. 133–140). Boston: Allyn & Bacon.

Gergen, P. J., Fowler, J. A., Maurer, K. R., Davis, W. W., & Overpeck, M. D. (1998). The burden of environmental tobacco smoke exposure on the respiratory health of children 2 months through 5 years of age in the United States: Third national health and nutrition examination survey, 1988–1994. Electronic abstracts: http://www.pediatrics.org.

Gesell, A., & Amatruda, C. S. (1941). *Developmental diagnosis: Normal and abnormal child development.* New York: Hoeber.

Gesell, A., & Ilg, F. L. (1949). *Child development.* New York: Harper and Row.

Ghazvini, A. S., & Readdick, C. A. (1994). Parent-caregiver communication and quality of care in diverse child care settings. *Early Childhood Research Quarterly, 9*(2), 207–222.

Golinkoff, R. M. (1983). The preverbal negotiation of failed messages: Insights into the transition period. In R. M. Golinkoff (Ed.), *The transition from prelinguistic to linguistic communication* (pp. 57–75). Hillsdale, NJ: Erlbaum.

Gottfried, A. (1984). Touch as an organizer of human development. In C. Brown (Ed.), *The many facets of touch* (pp. 114–120). Skillman, NJ: Johnson and Johnson.

Gottlieb, G. (1992). *Individual development and evolution: The genesis of novel behavior.* New York: Oxford University Press.

Gottlieb, G. (1995). Some conceptual deficiencies in 'developmental' behavior genetics. *Human Development, 38*(3), 131–141, 165–169.

Green, J. A., Jones, L. E., & Gustafson, G. E. (1987). Perception of cries by parents and nonparents: Relation to cry acoustics. *Developmental Psychology, 23,* 370–382.

Greenspan, S., & Greenspan, N. T. (1985). *First feelings.* New York: Penguin.

Grossmann, K., Grossmann, K. E., Spangler, G., Suess, G. L., & Unzner, L. (1985). Maternal sensitivity and newborns' orientation responses as related to quality of attachment in Northern Germany. In I. Bretherton & E. Waters (Eds.), Growing points of attachment theory and research. *Monographs of the Society for Research in Child Development, 50*(1–2, Serial No. 209, pp. 233–256).

Gunnar, M. R. (1996). *Quality of care and the buffering of stress physiology: Its potential in protecting the developing human brain.* University of Minnesota Institute of Child Development.

Haith, M. M. (1966). The response of human newborns to visual movement. *Journal of Experimental Child Psychology, 3,* 235–243.

Hall, G. S. (1893). *The contents of children's minds.* New York: Kellogg.

Hay, D. R., Nash, A., & Pederson, J. (1983). Interaction between six-month-old peers. *Child Development, 54,* 557–562.

Hooker, D. (1952). *The prenatal origin of behavior.* Lawrence: University of Kansas Press.

Hunt, C. E., & Brouillette, R. T. (1987). Sudden infant death syndrome: 1987 perspective. *Journal of Pediatrics, 110,* 669–678.

Hunziker, U. A., & Barr, R. G. (1986). Increased carrying reduces infant crying: A randomized controlled trial. *Pediatrics, 77,* 641–648.

Isabella, R. A. (1993). Origins of attachment: Maternal interactive behavior across the first year. *Child Development, 64*(2), 605–621.

Isabella, R. A., Belsky, J., & von Eye, A. (1989). Origins of infant-mother attachment: An examination of interaction synchrony during the infant's first year. *Developmental Psychology, 25,* (12–21).

Izard, C. E., & Buechler, S. (1986). Theoretical perspectives on emotions in developmental disabilities. In M. Lewis & L. Taft (Eds.), *Developmental disabilities: Theory, assessment, and intervention.* New York: Medical and Scientific Books.

Izard, C. E., Huebner, R., Risser, D., McGinness, G., & Dougherty, L. (1980). The young infant's ability to produce discrete emotion expressions. *Developmental Psychology, 16,* 132–140.

Jorgensen, M. H., Hernell, O., Lund, P., Hilmer, G., & Michaelsen, K. F. (1996). Visual acuity and erythrocyte docosahexaenoic acid status in breast-fed and formula-fed term infants during the first four months of life. *Lipids, 31*(1), 99–105.

Jusczyk, P. W., Cutler, A., & Redanz, N. J. (1993). Infants' preference for the predominant stress patterns of English words. *Child Development, 64*(3), 675–687.

Kagan, J. (1971). *Change and continuity in infancy.* New York: Wiley.

Kagan, J., Reznick, S., & Sniderman, N. (1988). Biological bases of childhood shyness. *Science, 240,* 167–171.

Kagan, J., Snidman, N., & Arcus, D. M. (1992). Initial reactions to unfamiliarity. *Current Directions in Psychological Science, 1,* 171–174.

Klahr, D., & Wallace, J. G. (1976). *Cognitive development: An information processing view.* Hillsdale, NJ: Erlbaum.

Klinnert, M. D., Campos, J. J., Sorce, J. F., Emde, R. N., & Svejda, M. (1983). Emotions as behavior regulators: Social referencing in infancy. In R. Plutchik & H. Kellerman (Eds.), *Emotion: Theory, research, and experience: Vol. 2. Emotions in early development* (pp. 57–86). New York: Academic Press.

Korner, A. F., Zeanah, C. H., Linden, J., Berkowitz, R. I., Kraemer, H. C., & Agras, W. S. (1985). The relation between neonatal and later activity and temperament. *Child Development, 56,* 38–42.

Lamb, M. E. (1978). The development of sibling relationships in infancy: A short-term longitudinal study. *Child Development, 49,* 1189–1196.

Lamb, M. E., Morrison, D. C., & Malkin, C. M. (1987). The development of infant social expectations, in face-to-face interaction: A longitudinal study. *Merrill-Palmer Quarterly, 33,* 241–254.

Lamme, L. L. (1980). Reading with an infant. *Childhood Education, 56,* 285–290.

Lewis, M. (1987). Social development in infancy and early childhood. In Osofsky, J. D. (Ed.). *Handbook of infant development,* 2nd ed., pp. 419–493. New York: Wiley.

Lewis, M., & Brooks-Gunn, J. (1979). *Social cognition and the acquisition of self.* New York: Plenum Press.

Lieberman, A. F., & Zeanah, C. Y. (1995). Disorders of attachment in infancy. *Infant Psychiatry, 4*(3), 571–587.

Locust, C. (1988). Wounding the spirit: Discrimination and traditional American Indian belief systems. *Harvard Educational Review, 58*(3), 315–329.

Lyons-Ruth, K., Alpern, L., & Repacholi, B. (1993). Disorganized infant attachment classification and maternal psychosocial problems as predictors of hostile-aggressive behavior in the preschool classroom. *Child Development, 64*(2), 572–585.

MacFarlane, A. (1977). *The psychology of childbirth.* Cambridge, MA: Harvard University Press.

Main, M., & Solomon, J. (1990). Procedures for identifying infants as disorganized/disoriented during the Ainsworth strange situation. In M. Greenberg, D. Cicchetti, & E. M. Cummings (Eds.), *Attachment in the preschool years: Theory, research, and intervention.* Chicago: University of Chicago Press.

Main, M., & Weston, D. R. (1981). The quality of the toddler's relationship to mother and father: Related to conflict behavior and the readiness to establish new relationships. *Child Development, 52,* 932–940.

Makin, J. W., & Porter, R. H. (1989). Attractiveness of lactating females' breast odors to neonates. *Child Development, 60,* 803–810.

Mandler, J. M. (1988). How to build a baby: On the development of an accessible representational system. *Cognitive Development, 3,* 113–136.

Mandler, J. M. (1990). A new perspective on cognitive development in infancy. *American Scientist, 78*(3), 236–243.

Mandler, J. M. (1992). Commentary on Bebko, Burke, Craven and Sario (1992): The importance of sensorimotor development: A perspective from children with physical handicaps. *Human Development, 36*(4), 226–240.

Mason, J. A., & Herrmann, K. R. (1998). Universal infant hearing screening by automated auditory brainstem response measurement. *Pediatrics, 101*(2), 221–228.

Mayhall, P., & Norgard, K. (1983). *Child abuse and neglect.* New York: Wiley.

Mehler, J. (1985). Language related dispositions in early infancy. In J. Mehler & R. Fox (Eds.), *Neonate cognition: Beyond the blooming buzzing confusion* (pp. 7–28). Hillsdale, NJ: Erlbaum.

Meltzoff, A. N., & Moore, M. K. (1983). Newborn infants imitate adult facial gestures. *Child Development, 54*(3), 702–709.

Meyerhoff, M. K. (1994), (March). Perspective on parenting: Crawling around. *Pediatrics for Parents,* pp. 8, 9.

Musick, J. S., & Householder, J. (1986). *Infant development: From theory to practice.* Belmont, CA: Wadsworth.

National Center for Children in Poverty. (1999). *Young children in poverty: A statistical update.* New York: National Center for Children in Poverty, Columbia University School of Public Health.

National Center for Health Statistics. (1994). *Vital and Health Statistics Series 20, No. 24,* DHHS Pub. No. (PHS) (94–1852). Hyattsville, MD: U.S. Department of Health and Human Services.

National Institutes of Health. (1993). Early identification of hearing impairment in infants and young children. *NIH Consensus Statement, 11*(1), 1–24.

Nelson, K. (1973). Structure and strategy in learning to talk. *Monographs of the Society for Research in Child Development, 38* (1–2, Serial No. 149).

Nelson, K. (1979). The role of language in infant development. In M. H. Bornstein & W. Kessen (Eds.), *Psychological development from infancy: Image to intention* (pp. 307–338). Hillsdale, NJ: Erlbaum.

Nelson, K., & Lucariello, J. (1985). The development of meaning in first words. In M. Barrett (Ed.), *Children's single word speech.* New York: Wiley.

Nizel, A. E. (1977). Preventing dental carries: The nutritional factors. In C. Neumann & D. B. Jelliffe (Eds.), *The pediatric clinics of North America* (Vol. 24, pp. 141–155).

Ogbu, J. U. (1981). Origins of human competence: A cultural ecological perspective. *Child Development, 52*(2), 413–429.

Olney, R., & Scholnick, E. (1976). Adult judgments of age and linguistic differences in infant vocalizations. *Journal of Child Language, 3,* 145–156.

Oster, H. & Ekman, P. (1977). Facial behavior in child development. In A. Collins (Ed.), *Minnesota Symposium on Child Psychology* (Vol. 11, pp 231–276). New York: Thomas A. Crowell.

Perry, B. (1993a). Neurodevelopmental and the neurophysiology of trauma I: Conceptional considerations for clinical work with maltreated children. *The Advisor, 6*(1), 1–2, 14–17.

Perry, B. (1993b). Neurodevelopmental and the neurophysiology of trauma. II: Clinical work along the alarm-fear-terror continuum. *The Advisor, 6*(1), 1–2, 14–18.

Perry, B. D. (1996). Incubated in terror: Neurodevelopmental factors in the 'cycle of violence.' In J. Osofsky (Ed.), *Children, youth, and violence: The search for solutions.* New York: Guilford Press.

Perry, B. (1998). *Brain growth and neurological development in infants.* Keynote presentation at the annual conference of the Texas Association for the Education of Young Children, Forth Worth, Texas.

Perry, B. D., Pollard, R. A., Blakley, T. L., Baker, W. L., & Vigilante, D. (1995). Childhood trauma, the neurobiology of adaptation, and 'use-dependent' development of the brain: How 'states' become 'traits.' *Infant Mental Health Journal, 16*(4), 271–291.

Piaget, J. (1926). *The language and thought of the child.* New York: Harcourt, Brace and World.

Piaget, J. (1952). *The origins of intelligence in children.* New York: Norton.

Pillitteri, A. (1992). *Maternal and child health nursing: Care of the childbearing and childrearing family.* Philadelphia: J. B. Lippincott.

Pinker, S. (1994). *The language instinct: How the mind creates language.* New York: Harper Perennial.

Plomin, R. (1987). Developmental behavioral genetics and infancy. In J. Osofsky (Ed.). *Handbook of infant development* (pp. 363–414). New York: Wiley.

Porter, F. L., Miller, R. H., & Marshall, R. E. (1986). Neonatal pain cries: Effect of circumcision on acoustic features and perceived urgency. *Child Development, 57,* 790–802.

Province, S., & Lipton, R. C. (1962). *Infants in institutions.* New York: International Universities Press.

Puckett, M. B., Marshall, C. S., & Davis, R. (1999). Examining the emergence of brain development research: The promises and the perils. *Childhood Education, 75* (7), 8–12.

Raikes, H. (1993). Relationship duration in infant care: Time with a high ability teacher and infant-teacher attachment. *Early Childhood Research Quarterly, 8*(3), 309–325.

Rosenthal, M. K. (1982). Vocal dialogues in the neonatal period. *Developmental Psychology, 18,* 17–21.

Ryan, C. A., & Finer, N. N. (1994). Changing attitudes and practices regarding local analgesia for newborn circumcision. *Pediatrics, 94*(2), 230–233.

Sameroff, A. J. (1983). Developmental systems: Contexts and evolution. In W. Kessen (Vol. Ed.), P. H. Mussen (General Ed.), Handbook of child psychology: Vol. 1. History, theory, and methods (4th ed). New York: Mosby.

Sameroff, A., & Chandler, M. J. (1975). Reproductive risk and the continuum of caretaking casualty. In F. D. Horowitz (Ed.), *Review of child development research,* (Vol. 4). Chicago: University of Chicago Press.

Samuels, C. A. (1985). Attention to eye contact opportunity and facial motion by three-month-old infants. *Journal of Experimental Child Psychology, 40,* 105–114.

Scheibel, A., Conrad, T., Perdue, S., Tomiyasu, U., & Wechsler, A. (1990). A quantitative study of dendrite complexity in selected areas of the human cerebral cortex. *Brain and Cognition, 12,* 85–101.

Shaffer, H. R. (1971). *The growth of stability.* London: Penguin.

Shiffrin, R. M., & Atkinson, R. C. (1969). Storage and retrieval processes in longterm memory. *Psychological Review, 76,* 179–193.

Shore, R. (1997). *Rethinking the brain: New insights into early development.* New York: Families and Work Institute.

Siegel, D. J. (1999). *The developing mind: Toward a neurobiology of interpersonal experience.* New York: Guilford Press.

Siegler, R. S. (1991). *Children's thinking* (2nd. ed.). Englewood Cliffs, NJ: Prentice Hall.

Skinner, B. F. (1938). *The behavior of organisms.* Englewood Cliffs, NJ: Prentice Hall.

Skinner, B. F. (1957). *Verbal behavior.* East Norwalk, CT: Appleton-Century-Crofts.

Skinner, B. F. (1974). *About behaviorism.* New York: Knopf.

Steiner, J. E. (1979). Human facial expressions in response to taste and smell stimulation. In H. Reese & L. Lipsitt (Eds.), *Advances in child development and behavior* (Vol. 13, pp. 257–295). New York: Academic Press.

Sternberg, R. J. (1985). *Beyond IQ: A triarchic theory of human intelligence.* New York: Cambridge University Press.

Stroufe, L. A. (1983). Infant caregiver attachments and patterns of adaptation in preschool: The roots of maladaptation and competence. In M. Perlmutter (Ed.), *Minnesota symposium on child psychology* (Vol. 16, pp. 41–81). Hillsdale, NJ: Erlbaum.

Sylwester, R. (1995). *A celebration of neurons: An educator's guide to the human brain.* Alexandria, VA: Association for Supervision and Curriculum Development.

Tanner, J. M. (1989). *Fetus into man: Physical growth from conception to maturity* (Rev. ed.). Cambridge, MA: Harvard University Press.

Thomas, A., & Chess, S. (1977). *Temperament and development.* New York: Brunner/Mazel.

Thomas, A., Chess, S., & Birch, H. G. (1968). *Temperament and behavior disorders in children.* New York: New York University Press.

Tronick, E. Z., Cohn, J., & Shea, E. (1986). The transfer of affect between mother and infant. In T. B. Brazelton & M. W. Yogman (Eds.), *Affective development in infancy* (pp. 11–25). Norwood, NJ: Ablex.

U.S. Department of Health and Human Services. (1990). *Healthy people 2000: National health promotion and disease prevention objectives.* DHHS Publication No. (DHS) 91-50213. Washington, DC: U.S. Government Printing Office.

Vaughn, V. C., III, & Litt, I. F. (1987). The newborn infant. In R. E. Behrman & V. C. Vaughn (Eds.), *Nelson textbook of pediatrics* (13th ed., pp. 7–17). Philadelphia: Saunders.

Vincent, J. D. (1990). *The biology of emotions,* (J. Hughes, Trans.). Cambridge, MA: Basil Blackwell.

Vygotsky, L. S. (1962). *Thought and language.* Cambridge, MA: MIT Press. (Original work published 1934)

Watson, J. B. (1924). *Behaviorism.* New York: Norton.

Weisner, T. (1982). Sibling interdependence and child caretaking: A cross cultural view. In M. E. Lamb & B. Sutton-Smith (Eds.), *Sibling relationships.* Hillsdale, NJ: Erlbaum.

Winnicott, D. W. (1971). *Playing and reality.* London: Tavistock Publications.

Wishart, J. G., & Bower, T. G. R. (1985). A longitudinal study of the development of the object concept. *British Journal of Developmental Psychology, 3,* 243–258.

Wolff, P. (1963). Observation on the early development of smiling. In B. Foss (Ed.), *Determinants of infant behavior* (Vol. 2, pp. 113–138). London: Methuen.

Wolff, P. H. (1966). The causes, controls, and organization of behavior in the neonate. *Psychology Issues, 5*(1, Serial No. 17).

Yarrow, L. (1961). Maternal deprivation: Toward an empirical and conceptual re-evaluation. *Psychological Bulletin, 58,* 459–490.